Share of MIND, Share of HEART

Marketing Tools of Engagement for Nonprofits

SYBIL F. STERSHIC

WME BOOKS
a division of
Windsor Media Enterprises, Inc.
Frederick, Colorado
USA

Share of Mind, Share of Heart
Marketing Tools of Engagement for Nonprofits

ISBN-10: 1-934229-34-2
ISBN-13: 978-1-934229-34-7

Editor: Yvonne DiVita
Cover Design: John Bartorillo, AJ Zambetti, and David Brodt
Back Cover Author Photo: Sally Ullman Photography
Page Layout/Design: Tom Collins

Published by:
WME Books
Windsor Media Enterprises, Inc.
Frederick, Colorado
USA

Available online at:
www.WMEBooks.com
as well as other booksellers and distributors worldwide.

Special Sales:
This and other WME Books titles are available at special discounts for bulk purchases, for use in sales promotions, or as premiums. Special editions, including co-branded covers, excerpts of existing books, and corporate imprints, can be created in large quantities for special needs or projects.

For more information, please contact:

Special Book Orders
Windsor Media Enterprises, Inc.
5412 Wolf Street
Frederick, CO 80504

Phone Toll-free:

1-877-947-BOOK (2665)

DEDICATION

In loving memory of my mother, Ruth H. Fischman.

CONTENTS

Acknowledgments v

Foreword vii

Part 1: Nonprofit Marketing and Engagement 1

Ch. 1. Understanding Nonprofit Marketing and Your Brand 3

Ch. 2. Why Nonprofit Marketing Needs to be Different but the Same 15

Ch. 3. Taking Care of the People Who Most Impact Your Brand 31

Part 2: Marketing Tools of Engagement 47

Ch. 4. Introduction to Internal Marketing Tools of Engagement 49

Ch. 5. Connecting to the Organization 57

Ch. 6. Connecting to Customers 71

Ch. 7. Connecting to Other Employees and Volunteers 81

Part 3: Facilitating Your Nonprofit Engagement 95

Ch. 8. Keeping People Engaged 97

Ch. 9. Making It Happen – Your Internal Marketing Plan 105

Afterword 119

Resources: Suggested Reading and Web Links 123

Index 125

About the Author 131

ACKNOWLEDGMENTS

I'm extremely fortunate to be associated with many dedicated nonprofit professionals and volunteers. While there are too many to name individually, they include my wonderful clients, the new and seasoned professionals who have attended my nonprofit workshops, and fellow volunteers with whom I served over the years. I am grateful for the privilege of working with and learning from them. Their passion and commitment inspire me.

Special thanks to my friends and colleagues who patiently listened as my ideas for this book took shape, especially Toby Bloomberg, Jon Dubbs, Dawn Lennon, Wayne McCullough, Debra Semans, Janet Tucker, and Andrea Weiss. In addition, special thanks go to the many professionals and volunteers who shared their stories, insights, and ideas about nonprofit engagement. I also want to acknowledge the members of my book critique group for their generous feedback, encouragement, and hospitality: Linda Reed Friedman, Celeste Behe, and Jack Hillman.

I am deeply grateful for the individual and collective efforts of the following who helped turn my manuscript into this beautiful book. Thanks to the wonderfully creative team at Maslow Lumia Bartorillo for designing my book cover: John Bartorillo, AJ Zambetti, and David Brodt. Special thanks to my dear sister,

Enid F. Gossin, and my dear friend, Charlotte Ravaioli, for taking the time to proof-read my manuscript. And to Yvonne DiVita and Tom Collins, my publishing team at Windsor Media Enterprises, my profound thanks for sharing your professional expertise and friendship in bringing this book to life.

I also want to acknowledge my "home" team for their ongoing support and good humor. I'm especially proud of my son, Jason, who is passionate about his work, both paid and volunteer.

I'm also fortunate to have a husband and partner, Michael, whose professional leadership I respect and who has forever captured my mind and heart.

FOREWORD

How it all started

My work with nonprofits started early. Before I could apply for a work permit at age 15, I spent a summer volunteering at a camp for intellectually disabled children. My mother had taught special education classes, so I was familiar with children who had Down Syndrome and other disabilities.

My volunteer experience that summer extended into the school year when I became involved with the local chapter of YOUTH ARC – Youth Organized & United To Help the Association for Retarded Children (as the ARC was known at the time) – a teen volunteer support group affiliated with the ARC. My peers and I assisted with local ARC fundraisers and awareness-building, recruited other teen volunteers, and helped organize holiday parties for the children and their families. I became deeply involved in the ARC by continuing to work at the summer camp, volunteering at a state-run residential "institution" for the mentally challenged, taking on a youth leadership role, and attending state and national YOUTH ARC conferences.

I also made a startling discovery about my involvement; compared with the other volunteers, I felt disheartened when I became frustrated working with the children. Truthfully, I didn't have the patience I felt was needed to be with them. Yet I enjoyed my involvement in ensuring the local YOUTH ARC was a viable organization, recruiting and mentoring the other young volunteers who were better suited to work with the kids. I discovered that people could serve in different capacities as long as they were passionate about the organization's mission.

That was the beginning of my love of working with nonprofits.

And now

Since then I've served a variety of nonprofits (including community service, healthcare, higher education, international services, professional associations and social services) in a range of roles: as a frontline volunteer, committee member, board member, board chair, and in a professional capacity as a marketing and organizational advisor.

Looking back over four decades of my personal and professional experience with nonprofits, I've learned three critical lessons:

1. ***Mission matters*** – it provides organizational focus and intention. It also brings together the people who share a passion for the mission and want to do something about it.
2. ***The people behind the mission also matter*** – these are the employees and volunteers who carry out the mission through their dedication and commitment.
3. ***People's passion for the mission should not be taken for granted*** – employees' and volunteers' passion for the mission does not guarantee their continued commitment to an organization.

I wrote this book to help nonprofit leaders, executives and managers more effectively engage the people behind the mission in their organizations.

How to use this book

Share of Mind, Share of Heart is a compact how-to guide that provides insight into the essence of nonprofit marketing and shares practical tools you can use to engage the people who most impact your brand.

"**Action Plan Starter Notes**" are included throughout the book to help you apply the content to your situation. Special worksheets found at the end of this book enable you to build on your notes and take the next step to create an internal marketing plan for your organization.

PART 1

Nonprofit Marketing and Engagement

CHAPTER 1 - Understanding Nonprofit Marketing and Your Brand

CHAPTER 2 - Why Nonprofit Marketing Needs to be Different but the Same

CHAPTER 3 - Taking Care of the People Who Most Impact Your Brand

CHAPTER 1

Understanding Nonprofit Marketing and Your Brand

> *Marketing really is spurred by the presence and the increase in competition that the institution faces in a way that it never faced before.*
>
> – Philip Kotler [1]

Marketing Spotlight: Goodwill Industries[2]

Have you ever cleaned out your closets to donate items to Goodwill®? Or shopped at a Goodwill store? While most people are familiar with Goodwill as shoppers and donors, they may not realize its overall mission is to serve communities by "eliminating barriers to opportunity and helping people in need reach their fullest potential through the power of work."

Goodwill Industries International pursues its mission through its network of more than 165 independent community-based Goodwill locations in the United States and Canada. These Goodwill organizations provide workforce development (such as job training and placement services) to people who have disabilities or those who lack education or job experience. It funds its efforts by selling donated items in its retail stores and online. As a mission-focused organization, Goodwill strives to operate effectively and efficiently while facing ever-increasing competition for donors and shoppers from:

- thrift shops run by other nonprofits
- privately run consignment shops
- discount retailers
- people who sell their used items through yard sales, Craig's List, and e-Bay.

How does Goodwill compete with both nonprofit and for-profit retailers? It manages its stores as professional, customer-focused retail operations that involve logistics, merchandising, and customer service. As a donor, I appreciate the positive and helpful reception I consistently get when I bring in items to my local Goodwill. It counters the negative experience I had with another nonprofit's thrift shop whose limited hours and limited staff made it a hassle to donate clothing and household items. Also, with the help of Goodwill's online calculator, I'm able to determine the tax deductible value of my donated items – a convenience I appreciate at tax time.

In addition, Goodwill targets select segments of shoppers by promoting its merchandise to suit their interests. For example, it highlights some of its stores or online offerings as a source of "vintage clothing" to appeal to younger, more upscale consumers while also maintaining its core base of low and middle income shoppers. Goodwill also reinforces shopper and donor involvement linking their efforts to its mission: in-store promotional signage explains that "every 42 seconds Goodwill places someone in a job." Users of Goodwill's website can calculate how their donations translate into career counseling hours.

Why Nonprofit Marketing?

With more than 1.2 million nonprofit organizations registered with the U.S. Internal Revenue Service, your nonprofit is literally one in a million.[3] This means you're in good company as an important sector of the economy. It also means you are competing with a vast number of other nonprofits – and sometimes, as in Goodwill's case, with for-profits – for resources and consumer attention.

Marketing can help you stand out in a crowded market and obtain the resources and attention you need to carry out your mission. Proactively marketing your nonprofit enables you to:

1. create an effective presence in the marketplace that helps differentiate you from competing organizations, and
2. pursue your mission through positive relationships with your stakeholders (consumers, members, volunteers, donors, referral sources, influencers, etc.)

My favorite description of nonprofit marketing's purpose came from an interview with management expert Peter Drucker and well-known marketing professor and author Philip Kotler. According to Kotler, marketing "is supposed to build up ... share of mind and share of heart for the organization." [4]

That quote best captures nonprofit marketing's essence. Here's what it means:

"Share of mind" (also referred to as "share of voice") is about creating and maintaining public awareness of your organization. *How can people support your organization and its mission if they don't know about you?*

"Share of heart" is creating and maintaining an emotional bond with people who are important to your organization. *Once people know about you, how will you build relationships with them and involve them in your nonprofit?*

A critical element of marketing is differentiating your organization in a crowded market so people know who you are and what you do, including your reputation for *how* you do what you do – in other words, your brand. Your nonprofit brand is a sum total of everything that goes into your organization's image; it determines whether or not people will want to engage with you. This is precisely why Goodwill doesn't treat donations at its retail locations as merely an operational function. It recognizes the critical role of staff who accept donations. These are the people who impact a new donor's first impressions and current donors' continued relationship with Goodwill.

You can differentiate your organization in a variety of ways. For example, you may have a unique mission or program offerings that are special in some way (i.e., better than those provided by other nonprofits). Staff expertise, quality operations, service excellence provided by staff and volunteers, and convenience (how accessible and/or easy you are to work with) are ways you can distinguish your organization. If you're not sure what positively sets you apart, ask your customers, staff, volunteers, and organizational partners: *"How are we different and better from other nonprofits?"*

It's easy to overlook the smallest things that make a difference. For example, one of my workshop attendees shared this anecdote about his social service agency. One day a representative of a grant-making foundation complimented his agency on having real people answer the phone instead of using automated voice mail. Given the amount of time foundation staff spent on the phone contacting the agencies they funded, this was important to them. Staff answering the phones was a point of differentiation the social service agency had not realized was so important.

An Important Note about Semantics

Donors are critical, of course, to those nonprofits that engage in fundraising. Since there are already numerous philanthropic management books and publications that address donor relations, this book focuses more on the people *who work in nonprofits* (employees and volunteers) and those who are *served by nonprofits* (consumers and customers). The latter group includes *nonpaying* consumers (e.g., those who receive free social, educational, or community services) as well as *paying* customers (e.g., government and institutional donors that support and/or subsidize such services).

While the term "customer" is commonly used in the for-profit sector, nonprofits use a variety of terms to describe the people they serve including:

- consumers
- clients
- stakeholders
- members
- patrons
- patients
- students
- congregants
- constituents, etc. (This list is not exhaustive.)

I use the generic terms "customer" and "consumer" interchangeably throughout this book to describe the people served by nonprofit organizations. If you're uncomfortable with any of these terms, please substitute the appropriate word(s) your nonprofit uses when thinking about those you serve.

Brand Power

Your brand is made up of many points of differentiation (real and imagined) that distinguish your nonprofit from similar organizations. A brand name immediately conjures up an organization's image and reputation. For example, what comes to mind when you think of the World Wildlife Fund? … Lance Armstrong Foundation? ... Salvation Army? Beyond immediate association with a symbol or color (a panda, a yellow bracelet, a red kettle), most consumers are familiar with these organizations and what they do.

The value of having a strong brand, one that is favorably perceived in the marketplace, is that it inspires trust and confidence in your organization. The stronger your brand, the more likely people will support and engage with your nonprofit – giving you their share of mind and heart.

Note: A program, event, or character can also be branded. While the public may not be familiar with the National Crime Prevention Council, its "Take a Bite Out of Crime®" campaign that features McGruff the Crime Dog® is well known.

Maintaining a strong brand involves constant oversight, as a brand is also fragile. While some nonprofits may (with appropriate handling) be able to survive an isolated scandal or public relations crisis, in today's highly networked world of social media, it doesn't take much to damage a brand. People can easily complain about your nonprofit through "word-of-mouse" that spreads faster and farther than ever before. That's why you need to care and protect your nonprofit brand.

As nonprofit consultant Elaine Fogel explains:

> "If we expect nonprofits to solve the problems that governments and businesses cannot fund, then it is in our collective best interest to ensure they function effectively. And if that means spending money to defend their brand assets, market their missions, and invest in things like leadership and staff development, it can only make them stronger and able to accomplish more." [5]

Who is Responsible for Marketing Your Brand?

Before answering this question, let's briefly explore marketing's broad scope. Nonprofit marketing covers a wide range of functions and activities that will vary by organization. These can include:

- product/service/program development
- promotion
- communications, publications, social media
- consumer/client/member services, development, and retention
- public relations, community relations, government relations
- special events planning and management
- fundraising/development, advancement, and donor relations
- volunteer recruitment, development, and retention.

Responsibility for these marketing-related activities may fall within the Marketing Department; a specific department named for the function itself (such as Communications, Programs, Member Services, etc.); or a broader area such as Community Outreach or Institutional Advancement. The departmental name and structure do not matter. How effectively these marketing tasks are carried out is far more important than where they are housed within an organization.

Even if marketing isn't recognized as a formal function on your organizational chart, your nonprofit still markets itself on a daily basis. Think about it: anytime people see or hear about activities your nonprofit is participating in or sponsoring – via any communication medium (newspaper article, poster, newsletter, email, Facebook, etc.) – they form an impression about you ("share of mind"). The resulting impression is positive, neutral, or negative.

Similarly, whenever people interact with your nonprofit – whether directly with a staff member (at one of your programs, volunteer orientation, fundraising gala, etc.) or indirectly (as the recipient of a phone call, fundraising solicitation, program brochure, or email) – each contact presents an opportunity to either develop a relationship ("share of heart") or damage it.

People also form impressions of your organization and decide whether or not they will get involved with you based on their interactions with your board of directors, volunteers, and even the consumers you serve. This is the reason organizations work hard to establish positive relationships with key stakeholders who serve as brand champions or advocates.

Given these almost limitless opportunities to impact share of mind and heart, *everyone in your organization is responsible for marketing!* So don't equate the absence of a formal marketing function with not doing any marketing.

The value of establishing and maintaining a formal marketing function (if it's feasible within your organization) is having an area dedicated to helping ensure that employee-customer interactions lead to positive share of mind and heart. For those of you fortunate to be in a formal marketing role, it's important to recognize that marketing's impact on your organization extends *outside* of your department.

An Introduction to Action Plan Starter Notes

This special section is designed to help you apply the information covered in this chapter. It is the first in a series of worksheets included throughout the book that will enable you to develop a plan to better engage your staff, volunteers, and ultimately, your consumers.

Marketing in My Nonprofit

Take a few minutes to respond to the following questions that explore marketing in your nonprofit organization. Answer these questions to the best of your ability. You can also share these questions with others in your organization for a collective response. The results will help you better understand marketing's current role in your nonprofit and what it may need going forward.

1. Briefly describe marketing in your organization. For example:

- Is it a formal or informal function?
- What is marketing's primary function (e.g., public relations, fundraising and development, community outreach, etc.)?
- Who shares marketing responsibility?
- How is marketing perceived in your nonprofit – is it considered a respected function, tolerated as a necessary evil, not given much thought, or just ignored?
- What else needs to be known about your organization's marketing function?

2. What organizations do you consider your primary competitors? Identify the organizations you compete with to acquire key resources such as funding, consumers/clients, volunteers, public attention, and any other needed resource(s) that enable you to pursue your mission. These may include:

- Nonprofits that have similar missions and/or provide services/programs that are similar to your organization's

- Nonprofits in general (if applicable)
- For-profits (if applicable)
- Other organizations (if applicable)

3. In what ways do you differentiate your nonprofit from these competitors? For example:

- How unique is your mission?
- Do you serve a special niche or provide special programs/services that few or no one else serves?
- How easy, accessible, convenient, etc., is your organization to work with?
- Do your staff and/or volunteers have special expertise?
- Other …

4. How would you rate your nonprofit's brand strength on the following scale?

1 2 3 4 5 6 7 8 9 10
Weak ← → Strong

Briefly explain your brand's placement on this scale.

Given your responses to these questions, what are your ideas to improve marketing's role and function in your organization?

Endnotes

1. Philip Kotler, in an interview with Peter F. Drucker, *Managing the Nonprofit Organization*, (New York, NY: Harper Collins, 1990), 80.
2. "About Goodwill Industries" http://www.goodwill.org/wp-content/uploads/2011/10/About-Goodwill-2011.pdf (accessed December 16, 2011)
3. National Center for Charitable Statistics, "Number of Nonprofit Organizations by State, 2010," http://nccsdataweb.urban.org/PubApps/profileDrillDown.php?rpt=US-STATE (accessed March 10, 2011).
4. Peter F. Drucker, *Managing the Nonprofit Organization*, op. cit.
5. Elaine Fogel, "How Far Should Charities Go to Protect Their Brands?", Marketing Profs Daily Fix Blog, February 7, 2011, http://www.mpdailyfix.com/how-far-should-charities-go-to-protect-their-brands/ (accessed February 9, 2011).

CHAPTER 2

Why Nonprofit Marketing Needs to be Different but the Same

Today, in any customer-facing organization, it's the people inside who deliver the brand experience that make the difference.... Their commitment and the experiences they deliver to customers shape and deliver the brand, and it is only through that commitment and those experiences that success occurs.

– Don E. Schultz and Heidi F. Schultz [1]

Your Service *is* Your Brand

As explained in the first chapter, the essence of nonprofit marketing is to build and sustain "share of mind" and "share of heart" for your organization. Your marketing success is based on not just what you do but also how you do it because you're marketing an intangible – be it community support, wellness, youth development, spiritual belonging, membership, education, or access to art & culture. In other words, you are a service provider whose service equates with your brand.

This chapter provides you with the necessary insight to better understand services marketing – and why it must be different, yet similar to traditional product marketing. First we'll explore how this type of marketing is different.

How Your Marketing Differs

Have you ever purchased a coffee maker or small kitchen appliance and discovered it didn't work after you took it out of the box? Perhaps you ordered a bookcase that required assembly but was missing a shelf or set of screws. After your initial frustration, consider the process you went through to remedy the situation. Consumers who find themselves with a defective new product typically return the item to the manufacturer or the store where it was purchased for a replacement product or credit. The product itself can be replaced, albeit with some degree of customer inconvenience.

What about a situation involving a defective service? For example, you sign in at a conference or fundraising event and the reception desk is unable to find your pre-paid registration. Frustration aside, a problem service encounter isn't something that you can simply return and replace (like a defective coffee-maker). This is one of the reasons that providing and marketing a "service" – which is what most nonprofits do – is significantly different than manufacturing and marketing a product.

Here is how services marketing differs from product marketing: [2]

- Services are intangible, mostly because they represent an experience. You cannot physically touch, handle, or return an experience.
- Services are created and consumed simultaneously. The coffee-maker is mass produced, ware-housed, and then shipped to either a retail store or a consumer's home after purchase. The person who attends an educational event (on-site or virtual) or a fundraising gala is directly involved in the experience as it happens.
- Services are time-perishable. The coffee-maker can sit on the store shelf until it is purchased; if unsold, it doesn't disappear. Yet an empty seat during a community concert performance or the fundraising dinner represents an unsold ticket and lost revenue that cannot be reclaimed.
- Services are of uneven quality due to human factors. You may not care that one of the employees who worked on the coffee-maker production line was having a bad day, as long as quality assurance standards are in place. You will feel the difference, however, when you interact with a volunteer coordinator who has a negative attitude.

Understanding What's Important from Your *Customer's* Perspective

Marketing a service rather than a product is more challenging because of its intangible, experiential nature. Regardless of what it is you market – whether it's a special cause, health and wellness, membership, education, social and/or community well-being, the arts, or other nonprofit offering – it's imperative to understand the service experience and what's important to the customer from the *customer's* perspective.

To understand this concept, consider your own experience as a customer dining out at a restaurant. Have you ever been to a restaurant that had wonderful food, but lousy service? Or, perhaps you were treated to excellent service, but the meal itself was mediocre. In either situation, would you recommend that restaurant? Most people will speak positively of a restaurant with both excellent food and service.

This example highlights two critical aspects of a restaurant customer's service experience:

1. The **outcome** or result of the overall meal – did you enjoy dining out?
2. The **process** that consists of a myriad of interactions leading to the outcome. This includes how you were treated when you called to make your dinner reservation; the availability and convenience of parking; how long you waited to be seated; restaurant staff friendliness and responsiveness; the restaurant's decor and ambience; menu variety; how long you waited to place your drink and menu order; food and beverage quality; restroom cleanliness; how long you waited to receive and pay your bill; and how you were acknowledged for your patronage.

Similarly, your nonprofit customers evaluate specific details of their interactions and overall experience with your organization. For example, customers who attend a special event or meeting hosted by your nonprofit are affected by how they are treated by your staff during the registration process, including answering questions about the event; how easy it is to find the venue and parking availability; the appearance and cleanliness of the meeting/event space; on-site welcome and/or reception; the perceived value of the event or meeting itself; etc. Together these individual and cumulative interactions influence what the customer thinks of your brand.

To better manage the process and outcome of a customer's experience, we need to understand how customers evaluate the quality of service provider interactions. Research shows that consumers judge service quality using the following five attributes.[3]

- **Reliability** – the ability to provide what was promised dependably, accurately, and consistently.
  Does your organization deliver what it promises?
- **Assurance** – the employees' ability to convey trust and confidence with the people they serve.
  Is your staff courteous, knowledgeable, and competent?
- **Tangibles** – the appearance of staff, physical facilities, equipment, and materials used in service delivery (e.g., reports and related handout materials).
  Do the people and tangible items associated with your service(s) convey a quality impression that reflects positively on your brand?
- **Empathy** – the degree of caring, individualized attention provided to customers.
  How does your staff show customers that they understand their needs?
- **Responsiveness** – the willingness to provide prompt service and help customers.
  When a customer has a concern or problem, how attentive is staff to helping address and/or resolve the situation?

Here's a personal example of how a member-based organization lost me as a customer by performing poorly on several of these service quality attributes. I was excited when I first joined a membership organization that serves leaders in the nonprofit field. My paid membership fee gave me access to an online newsletter, discounted publications, and an annual conference designed for idea-exchange and networking. But after a year I decided not to renew my membership as I felt I hadn't gotten much benefit out of it. It was only when working on my membership budget that I realized I hadn't received a renewal notice. I also never received the quarterly journal promised in the membership material, and the organization had been unresponsive when I emailed staff questions about one of their events.

So I was surprised when I got a letter telling me my membership was extended for one year. I e-mailed the organization to ask why – given my work as a nonprofit consultant, I was curious. Was the membership offer a matter of recovering a lost member? Or did the group have such a great year that they decided to "share the wealth" with their membership?

After several weeks with no response, I sent a letter to the organization's board chair, including a copy of my earlier e-mail. Within a few days, I received a voice mail and letter from a staff member with an apology and an explanation. The explanation was based on insufficient staffing and miscommunication with the members. I found the apology acceptable and the explanation lame.

Member-based organizations, no matter how well intentioned their missions, won't survive without members. Such groups need to pay attention to the member/customer experience, and I'm not talking about anything complicated here – just the basics of delivering what was promised (Reliability), communicating effectively to manage member expectations (Assurance) and answering member questions and concerns in a timely manner (Responsiveness).

While most of the service quality attributes evaluate the intangible and experiential nature of a service encounter, keep in mind the importance of any tangible items associated with a service – their impact should not be underestimated. Here's another personal example, and it's based on when my mother was admitted to a hospital with chest pains. She was visibly upset when I met her at the hospital, and her panic went beyond the fear of a possible heart attack.

My mother showed me a document about hospital rules and procedures that she received upon admission to the hospital – a document in which she found over a dozen typos. My mother was a retired English teacher. (You know the type who never went anywhere without a red pen?) However, because she was a teacher and not a cardiac specialist, she was unable to assess the quality of cardiac care she would receive. What she could evaluate was the quality of caring she expected to receive based on the tangible cues she found in the poorly written document. "If the hospital is this careless with a simple handout," she told me, "how do I know they won't be careless with me?"

To a hospital administrator, that tangible item may have been just a simple handout with a few typos, produced by a clerk and distributed as part of the admissions process. To my mother, the patient, it was a carelessly produced document that negatively impacted her assurance in hospital staff and her perceived expectation of care.

As a nonprofit marketing an intangible service, it's important to pay close attention to your customer's overall experience - including any tangible elements that are part of that experience.

Why Your Marketing Must be the Same

Marketing your nonprofit brand involves creating both brand awareness and brand meaning.[4]

a. **Brand awareness** is how you position, package, and promote your nonprofit through marketing communications – via your logo, paid and/or public service advertising, public relations, direct marketing, website, social media, community outreach efforts, etc.

b. **Brand meaning** is the consumer's take-away impression of your nonprofit based on the person's experience with your organization.

In essence, brand awareness is what you promise and brand meaning is what consumers think of you based on how that promise is delivered. There may be times your communications convey a message and set expectations that do not match what the customer actually experiences. So it's necessary to align what you promise with what you deliver. Or ensure you set realistic expectations (via marketing communications) so that you only deliver what you promise. This is where your marketing must be the same; i.e., your marketing messages need to be consistent with your organization's actions.

Let's go back to the example I shared earlier about my mother's hospital experience. The hospital marketed itself within the community using outdoor, television, and newspaper advertising; direct mail; and the hospital's website to promote its quality healthcare specialties. It also was active in the community, partnering with a number of health-related and educational nonprofits to advocate wellness. While the hospital's marketing created public expectations of quality healthcare, its poorly produced Admissions handout contradicted this message of quality and negatively affected my mother's perception of the hospital's brand. We will never know how many other patients felt the same way!

Achieving consistency with the brand promise and its delivery can be tricky given the number and variety of "brand touch points" between your nonprofit and your customer. A touch point is any contact the customer has with your organization: face-to-face, word-of-mouth, or any other form of communication medium (traditional and/or electronic) that conveys a message about your brand and sets customer expectations.

Brand Contacts

Marketing
Communications

Brochures
Letters/e-mail
Requests
Annual Reports
PR
Website
Social Media
Other ...

Special Events

Fundraisers
Recognition
Open House
Orientation
Webinar
Other ...

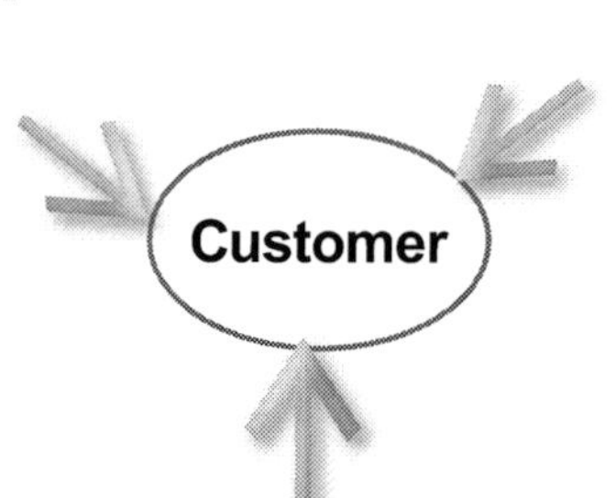

Other Contact

Meetings
Programs
Phone calls
Reports
On-site Reception
Gift Shop
Other ...

Any time customers come into contact with some aspect of your organization (through one or more touch points), they use it as an opportunity to judge the quality of your nonprofit brand. All touch points need to carry the same marketing message – whatever you communicate must be consistent with how you follow through in your interactions with customers. This makes it critical to consider how your organization manages its brand touch points.

Effectively managing these brand contacts is a challenge, especially when they may fall outside your scope of authority. This situation reinforces the fact that everyone in your organization is involved in marketing, regardless of what's listed on their job descriptions. We'll explore employees' impact on your brand in the next chapter.

Action Plan Starter Notes

Application:
Improving Your Customer's Experience

Take a few minutes to consider how you can improve the service quality of your customer's interactions with this exercise. Please note: You can choose to use an actual experience that happened in your organization or consider how a typical situation would play out.

1. Identify a type of person who is important to your organization – such as a client, member, community partner, referral source, etc. – **and a situation** this person would likely be involved in with your nonprofit. For example: A new client intake meeting, mentor training, new member orientation, recognition or educational event, etc.

Briefly describe here:

> **Person** (instead of a specific individual's name, please describe the person at the center of this scenario, such as a client, referral source, patron, board member, etc.)

Situation

2. **Describe a positive or ideal outcome** of this situation; i.e., what would you like to happen as a result of this situation?

Outcome/Results

3. Objectively visualize and note the process this person would go through in this situation. Consider:

Who is the person interacting with? How many different people from your organization will the person encounter in this situation? Who else is involved?

Where is the interaction taking place? In what setting are they meeting?

How is this person being treated as s/he goes through the process? Is the person given the all the information needed in this interaction? How is this information being explained? Is sufficient time allowed? What else is happening in this interaction that will impact this person?

Imagine how this person might evaluate the quality of his/her experience using the attributes of Reliability, Assurance, Tangibles, Empathy, and Responsiveness (described earlier in this chapter). Then consider how this person is likely to evaluate the overall experience.

4. Now step back and review the experience from your perspective as a service provider.

Which of the attributes did you do well on?

Which attributes concern you?

What insights do you take away from this exercise?

I encourage you to share this chapter and its exercise with your staff to stimulate discussion on how to improve the process and outcomes of the customer's service experience.

Application:
Aligning Marketing and Brand Touch Points

You can also solicit staff input and ideas here.

1. **Select one stakeholder group to start with,** such as clients, key referral sources, board members, etc., and identify all possible brand touch points your nonprofit has with that segment.

2. **What can your organization do to ensure consistency** among these brand touch points?

Endnotes

1. Don E. Schultz and Heidi F. Schultz, *Brand Babble: Sense and Nonsense About Branding* (Mason, OH: Thomson South-Western, 2004): 26.
2. Adapted from Valarie A. Zeithaml, A. Parasuraman, and Leonard L. Berry, "Problems and Strategies in Services Marketing," *Journal of Marketing* 49 (Spring 1985): 33-46.
3. Leonard L. Berry and A. Parasuraman, *Marketing Services* (New York, NY: The Free Press, 1991): 16.
4. Leonard L. Berry, *Discovering the Soul of Service* (New York, NY: The Free Press, 1999): 200.

CHAPTER 3

Taking Care of the People Who Most Impact Your Brand

"… the key to building a nonprofit brand and cause with legs is to establish a powerful emotional connection with people and then give them ways to meaningfully engage …"

– Emily Callahan [1]

Mission Matters ... To a Point

What is unique about nonprofits is that they are so mission-focused. When you're passionate about your mission, it's easier to feel good about your work. But having a noble mission doesn't guarantee organizational success!

Effectively managing a nonprofit is a challenge that involves developing and maintaining good relationships with the board, staff and volunteers; planning and delivering mission-based programs to meet constituent needs; securing resources and funding; ensuring governance compliance; etc. With so many responsibilities, it's easy for nonprofit managers to get caught up in operational issues and lose sight of what matters – and what matters is the tremendous impact every employee and volunteer has on your organization's brand.

As a service-based organization, everyone who works and volunteers in your nonprofit has a marketing role in delivering on your brand promise via a variety of touch points – through interactions in meetings and special events, as well as through all forms of communication with stakeholders and the community-at-large. Remember, whenever consumers come into contact with your nonprofit (whether directly or indirectly), they use it as an opportunity to judge your brand. So the degree to which you capture and keep consumers' share of mind and heart is directly influenced by their interactions with your staff and volunteers.

Engagement Matters

Your best efforts to advance your mission by creating a favorable impression of your nonprofit depend upon how engaged your employees and volunteers are in supporting your organization. But what exactly is workplace engagement? While a popular management topic, people have difficulty articulating what engagement really means.

An easy way to understand employee engagement comes from research firm BlessingWhite's description of the difference between employees who are engaged and those who are not: Engaged employees stay for what they give – they like their work and are able to contribute, whereas disengaged employees stay for what they get – a comfortable job, good salary, and decent job conditions.[2] *Who would you rather have work in your organization?*

Because their work is mission-driven, nonprofit employees can be presumed to be more engaged than employees who work in the for-profit sector but are not necessarily so (depending on the organization's culture). Research suggests a nonprofit employee's passion for the mission may not be enough to sustain his/her on-the-job engagement.[3] "This varies by organization," according to Bill McEwen, Customer Engagement Practice Leader for Evolve Performance Group and former Gallup consultant, "as some [managers] are super in recognizing and energizing those who work for them, while others may pay great attention to their mission and relatively little attention to the people called upon to fulfill it."[4] Sadly, I'm familiar with nonprofits whose employees became disenchanted and disengaged because their workplace was poorly managed, even toxic. Any organization oblivious to low morale and high turnover risks brand disintegration.

Note: The term "employee engagement" throughout this chapter refers to engaging all the people who work in your organization – paid employees and unpaid volunteers.

Marketing from the Inside Out

If you're fortunate to have a workforce of skilled employees and volunteers who believe in your brand, how do you engage them and keep them engaged? You start by recognizing them as your most important internal audience – especially given their individual and collective impact on your nonprofit brand. Before you can effectively market to consumers, you need to market to your employees and volunteers. An "inside-out marketing" approach enables you to take care of these internal stakeholders so they can take care of your external stakeholders: clients, customers, members, donors, referral sources, corporate and community partners, etc. Applying marketing inside your organization addresses both the rational and emotional sides of employee engagement:

- Rationally engaged employees and volunteers "understand how their work contributes to the success of the organization"
- Emotionally engaged employees and volunteers "feel inspired to do their best."[5]

Think of it this way: you can apply marketing to engage the hearts and minds of your internal stakeholders just as you use it to engage the hearts and minds of your external stakeholders.

Internal marketing, as I'll now refer to the concept, is "the ongoing process whereby an organization aligns, motivates, and empowers employees at all functions and levels to consistently deliver a positive customer experience that helps achieve business objectives."[6] Internal marketing is basically a strategic blend of marketing, human resources, and management to ensure employees and volunteers have the information, tools, and support they need to be actively engaged in your nonprofit. It establishes and reinforces a clear "line of sight" from employee/volunteer input to organizational output on three separate (yet overlapping) levels of understanding.

- **Organizational Understanding**
  Do your employees and volunteers know the organization's mission, strategy, and goals? Do they know what is expected of them in helping your organization achieve its goals? Do they understand how their individual and collective efforts impact mission fulfillment?
- **Customer/Stakeholder Understanding**
  How well do employees and volunteers know who your organization's customers/stakeholders are, what is important to them, and why they choose to be involved with your nonprofit? Is customer feedback (from satisfaction surveys and/or complaint tracking) collected and shared internally? How involved are your employees and volunteers in improving stakeholder satisfaction?
- **Employee/Volunteer Understanding**
  Do employees and volunteers know how their actions impact customers? (This includes working with fellow employees/volunteers who are "internal" customers.) Do they have the right skills and tools needed to take care of customers and co-workers? How do your staff and volunteers know they are valued by the organization?

Internal marketing addresses these concerns with a range of intentional and integrated organizational activities including (but not limited to) training, recognition, reinforcement, empowerment, information sharing, and team building. Collectively these activities reinforce the value of staff/volunteers and the stakeholders they serve.

Note: Despite its name, internal marketing falls within the domain of all leaders and managers, regardless of their functional responsibility. Just because you're not in marketing or human resources doesn't mean you shouldn't be applying internal marketing.

Internal Marketing Strategy – The 3 Rs Foundation

To gain employee and volunteer commitment and facilitate their engagement with an organization, internal marketing strategy is based on what I call the "Three Rs Formula":

- **Respect** – ensure your staff members and volunteers have the necessary tools and support to do their work.
- **Recognition** – catch them doing something right.
- **Reinforcement** – continually support a mission-based, customer-focused culture.

Engaging Employees & Volunteers with Respect

An organization respects its employees and volunteers when it gives them the proper information and support they need to perform their jobs. Respect is applied by communicating with, training, and empowering them to do their best in serving the organization and its customers.

Communication

Tell employees/volunteers what your nonprofit is all about – its mission, direction, strategy and goals – and what is expected of them in accomplishing the goals and furthering the mission. This helps them understand what your organization is trying to achieve and how they can effectively contribute to the outcome. Giving your staff/volunteers this information – i.e., what their roles are in the "big picture" – is critical to your nonprofit's success, as it's "only when [workers] understand how they fit into the bigger picture … that they can apply the discretionary effort necessary for the organization overall to excel."[7] *How can your employees and volunteers help your nonprofit move forward if they don't know where the organization is going and what is expected of them?*

Open communication from management and across organizational silos ensures that your people have access to the information and knowledge they need to perform their jobs. Employees and volunteers need answers to basic questions such as:

1. What is our organization's mission, where are we headed, and what is expected of us?
2. What capacity and resources do we have to reach the organization's goals?
3. What do we need to know and do to help us achieve these goals?

Employees, specifically, need to know about:

- Future plans, strategic direction, and goals for the organization
- The rationale behind important management decisions and actions
- Competitive, economic, legislative, and other relevant marketplace impacts
- Customer/stakeholder feedback
- Service performance and new program or service development
- Operating guidelines, policies, and performance standards
- Benefits and promotion opportunities.[8]

Sharing such basic information with staff seems like a no-brainer, yet many organizations (nonprofit as well as for-profit) fall short in communicating this vital content to employees. Perhaps managers are so focused on doing their own work they presume their employees already know this information or will seek it out as needed. It may also be that because this information is so basic it tends to fall through the organizational cracks. Regardless of the reason, according to communications consultant/ author Bill Quirk: "When employees understand their overall role in the business, 91% will work towards success, but the number plummets to 23% if they don't."[9] Jan Carlzon, former president of Scandinavian Airlines Systems (SAS), understood this and made it part of his personal leadership philosophy: "An individual without information cannot take responsibility; an individual who is given information cannot help but take responsibility."[10]

Training

Another critical component of Respect involves providing opportunities for people to develop and/or enhance the skills necessary to perform their jobs. Multiple levels of employee training may be required, ranging from functionally-related training (how to do a particular job, as well as maintain any necessary accreditation) to supervisory/management training.

A training and development checklist should also include the following:

- **Orientation** – whether formal or informal, it's important to introduce all new employees and volunteers to your organization and make them feel welcome as valued members of the team. Special attention may be needed for staff hired from the for-profit sector to help them adapt to the nonprofit world.
- **"Product" knowledge** – employees and volunteers need to be familiar with the services and programs your nonprofit offers, including any new "product" developments or changes to existing offerings. Depending on the size and scope of your organization, staff/volunteers not directly involved in service/program delivery may not need detailed training here. At a minimum, however, they should be briefed on all your offerings, including who is responsible for them, so they know where to direct any referrals, questions, or related problems. You want to avoid this situation experienced by a frustrated social worker. She told me about working in a social service agency where "different parts

of the agency didn't know how to put the pieces together." As a result, staff regularly referred clients to another agency when these clients could have been served in-house!

- **Communications and customer relations skills** – the general public considers your employees and volunteers to be the "face" of your organization. As such, they need to possess and build on basic interpersonal skills to deal with stakeholders and each other. When your clients, donors, or members contact your organization by phone, what impression are they likely to get from the employee or volunteer answering the phone? Is it the same impression you want them to take away from that call? If a stakeholder or co-worker has a complaint, what is the appropriate way for employees to respond and/or recover this situation? Does your organization provide the necessary training, support and reinforcement that equip staff and volunteers to effectively interact with your stakeholders and the public-at-large?

  Given the public's appetite for social media, do the messages your staff or volunteers send on LinkedIn, Twitter, and Facebook reflect positively or negatively on your nonprofit? Even with limited training resources, you can use internal media (email or newsletters, employee handbooks, operating guidelines, etc.) and staff meetings to model and reinforce professional behavior in effectively communicating and interacting with people – both online and offline.

Empowerment

Besides equipping your people with proper information about your organization and the appropriate job training, you also need to give them the latitude to perform their jobs without micromanaging their every step. It's difficult to be excited and engaged about work when managers are constantly hovering over you. This does not mean that all employees and volunteers are given free rein to do whatever they choose. Empowerment means your people are enabled and allowed to do the work they are asked to do without being micromanaged or hampered by unnecessary interference.

Effective and ongoing communication, training, and empowerment form the cornerstone of Respect. An easy way to remember these elements is explaining, training, and refraining:

- ***Explaining*** where employees/volunteers fit within the scope of the organization and what's expected of them
- ***Training*** them to do their jobs, and
- ***Refraining*** from getting in their way.

Engaging Employees & Volunteers with Recognition

Recognition is the second R in the "3Rs Formula" to obtain staff/volunteer commitment and engagement. Whenever possible, catch your people doing something right! While many nonprofits spend time and attention recognizing their donors and volunteers, they don't necessarily extend the same effort to their employees.

Recognition need not be extravagant – it can be as simple as sincere acknowledgment for a job well done, delivered verbally or in writing, formally or informally. It can also be fun, such as surprising an individual or group of employees with pizza, popcorn, or other special treat. (Never underestimate the power of food in an office setting. Bring in delectable goodies and you can set off a feeding frenzy!)

Many nonprofits utilize a variety of methods to recognize their employees and volunteers. For example, the Jewish Family & Career Services of Atlanta (JF&CS) hosts an annual Staff Appreciation Week for its 200+ employees in which the senior management team and the staff development committee treat employees to special breaks with breakfast, baked goods, ice-cream, and other snacks throughout the week. Employees of this community service organization also enjoy a holiday "mocktail" party in December with food and non-alcoholic beverages served by members of senior management who dress in costume for the event.

JF&CS recognizes its volunteers in a special "Volunteer Spotlight" column in the nonprofit's monthly e-newsletter. Volunteer accomplishments are also acknowledged at board meetings to which the honored volunteer is invited. In addition, formal recognition for meritorious service is awarded to an employee and a volunteer at the organization's annual meeting. According to Brenda Fiske, Chief Marketing Officer, staff and volunteer appreciation are part of JF&CS's commitment to talent management, a strategic priority that reflects "the services we provide are only as good as the people who provide them."[11]

Such highly visible recognition events and celebrations are an integral part of how organizations instill pride in performance and contribute to an emotionally committed workforce.[12] Beyond fun or formal ceremony, recognition is more than just special awards – it acknowledges the importance of people's work and makes them feel valued. Unfortunately, it isn't always applied that way. Think of workplace recognition as a form of positive reinforcement. In many organizations, positive reinforcement is a lack of negative reinforcement – if you didn't get your hand slapped today for doing something wrong, you might have done a good job. But how would you know if no one ever tells you? This is the reason it's important to catch your people doing something right!

Engaging Employees & Volunteers with Reinforcement

Reinforcement, the third "R" of employee commitment and engagement, involves continually supporting a mission-driven, customer-focused culture. A nonprofit has numerous internal communication vehicles to demonstrate and reinforce the importance of pursuing its mission and developing positive customer relationships via:

- All-employee meetings and smaller staff meetings (depending on the organization's size)
- Volunteer meetings and get-togethers
- Internal newsletters (print and electronic)
- Employee and volunteer recognition
- Staff/volunteer appreciation events
- Staff/volunteer development and/or planning retreats
- Signage – such as Goodwill's promotional posters that link donor and shopper involvement with its mission.

A note of caution here: you can disseminate well thought-out and creative messages about taking care of your stakeholders and mission, but it is wasted effort if the words are empty rhetoric. For example, employees watch for behavioral cues as to whether leaders' and managers' actions support these messages; i.e., do they "walk the talk?" A manager who says volunteers are important, yet avoids any contact with them, sends a mixed message to staff. Credibility and consistency are critical to effective reinforcement.

Here's how one nonprofit, a professional association, combines Respect, Recognition, and Reinforcement in one event. At the beginning of its new fiscal year in early July, the organization closes its office for the day to hold a special staff retreat. The morning session consists of an annual meeting in which senior managers and department representatives give progress reports on the association's results for the past year. The chief staff executive then shares strategic goals and objectives for the coming year. The organization's board chairperson also gives his/her leadership message and reinforces the staff's role in serving the association's members and chapters. The morning session concludes with staff awards for service excellence and goal achievement presented by the chief staff executive and board chair. The staff retreat continues in the afternoon with lunch and a fun team-bonding experience at an amusement park, museum, or baseball game.

The 3 Rs of employee commitment and engagement come together in this example. The association shows respect for its employees for taking the time to review and recognize the past year's accomplishments and share its plans and priorities for the new year. Top management and the board chair recognize the staff's individual and collective achievements and reinforce the association's mission and staff-member partnership. Closing the office for one day to engage in business and fun is an investment in staff that reinforces the message employees matter.

We'll explore how other nonprofits apply the 3Rs in the next several chapters as we move from a general framework to specific internal marketing tools you can use to engage your employees and volunteers.

Action Plan Starter Notes

Instructions:

Take a few minutes to identify how your organization applies each of the 3 Rs in gaining staff and volunteer commitment and facilitating their engagement. List all current and planned activities, efforts, and events that relate to Respect, Recognition, and Reinforcement. It's possible that some initiatives may overlap in two or more Rs.

1. How does your organization show **Respect:**

For employees

For volunteers

2. How does your organization **Recognize** the following for a job well done:

Employees

Volunteers

3. How does your organization **Reinforce** a mission-driven, stakeholder focused culture:

Among employees

Among volunteers

Endnotes

1. Emily Callahan in a *Marketing News* interview about her role as chief marketing officer of ALSAC, the fundraising organization for St. Jude Children's Research Hospital, January 30, 2011, 30.
2. BlessingWhite, Inc., *The State of Employee Engagement 2008 – North American Overview*, v.04/08, 1.
3. "Who is More Engaged: Nonprofit or For-profit Employees?" *Quality Service Marketing Blog*, May 19, 2009. http://qualityservicemarketing.blogs.com/quality_service_marketing/2009/05/nonprofit-employee-engagement-it-takes-more-than-the-mission.html
4. Ibid.
5. "Employee Lifetime Value: 'The People Impact' on Financial Success," Forum for People Performance Management and Measurement, http://www.performanceforum.org/associations/12672/files/employee_lifetime_value_people_impact.pdf, 2008.
6. "Internal Marketing Best Practice Study," Forum for People Performance Management and Measurement, http://www.performanceforum.org/Internal_Marketing_Best_Practice_Study.63.0.html, 2006.
7. Nancy S. Alrichs, *Competing for Talent: Key Recruitment and Retention Strategies for Becoming an Employer of Choice* (Palo Alto: Davies-Black Publishing, 2000) 176.
8. Adapted from Sybil F. Stershic, *Taking Care of the People Who Matter Most* (WME Books, 2007), 22-23.
9. Bill Quirk, *Making the Connections: Using Internal Communication to Turn Strategy into Action* (Hampshire, England: Gower Publishing Ltd, 2008) 11.
10. Carol Sturman, "Dare to Dream," *Leader to Leader*, 23 (Winter 2002) 35-39.
11. Interview with Brenda Fiske, Chief Marketing Officer, Jewish Family & Career Services of Atlanta, Inc., January 11, 2012.
12. Jon R. Katzenbach, *Why Pride Matters More than Money* (NY: Crown Business, 2003), 147-149.

Part 2

Marketing Tools of Engagement

CHAPTER 4 - Introduction to Internal Marketing Tools of Engagement

CHAPTER 5 - Connecting to the Organization

CHAPTER 6 - Connecting to Customers

CHAPTER 7 - Connecting to Other Employees and Volunteers

CHAPTER 4

Introduction to Internal Marketing Tools of Engagement

> Connection is the key. When we disconnect, we disengage.
>
> – David Zinger [1]

In my previous book on internal marketing, *Taking Care of the People Who Matter Most: A Guide to Employee-Customer Care*, I presented two sets of internal marketing tools to engage employees. Both are based on the **3Rs Foundation** of ***Respect***, ***Recognition***, and ***Reinforcement***. These tools impact the relationship between employees and customers (the "Employee-Customer Link") and the relationship among employees (the "Internal Service Culture").

This book adapts and expands these tools to better enable nonprofit organizations to strengthen both employee and volunteer relationships with:

- the organization and its mission (Internal Service Culture),
- the consumers served by the organization (the Employee-Customer Link), and
- fellow co-workers – other staff and volunteers within the organization (Internal Service Culture).

Connected and Engaged

The three sets of internal marketing tools prescribed here will enable you to build and reinforce a stronger "'Connection Culture' where people feel connected to their organization's identity … to the people they work alongside … their work tasks … and to the organization's decisions."[2] This type of culture is based on "engaging people in authentic and recognized connections to strategy, roles, performance, organization, community, relationship, customer, development, energy, and happiness to leverage, sustain, and transform work into results."[3]

A strong sense of connection is important in engaging people in their work. To be engaged, people want:

- To be part of something big, something special, where their work is associated with a "sense of substance, importance, pride and direction"
- To feel a sense of belonging
- To go on a meaningful journey where their work is invested in something that matters
- To know that their contributions make a significant impact or difference; i.e., that their efforts matter.[4]

These reasons also underscore that employee engagement is a joint responsibility. While management's role is to create and maintain an engaged culture, the employees and volunteers who work there are equally responsible for their own engagement. As author and engagement expert Richard Axelrod explains, "A mistake some organizations make is that they think it's a kind of plug-and-play ... we can mechanically set up all this engagement stuff and then people will automatically become engaged. That doesn't happen. What you can do is set up the conditions whereby people might choose to become engaged. Engagement is ... a two-way choice. The leadership in an organization has to choose to adopt this sort of strategy, and then the employee [and volunteer] has to choose to join in."[5]

Managers at The Wounded Warrior Project in Jacksonville, FL, know that maintaining an engaged and connected workplace is based on their ability to create an environment where employees know they are cared about. The organization ranked first in The *NonProfit Times* "50 Best Nonprofits to Work For in 2011" list. According to Steven Nardizzi, CEO of The Wounded Warrior Project, "Our staff is tremendous at fulfilling its mission every day, and we try to empower them and treat them the way we would want to be treated."[6]

Disconnected and Disengaged

Sadly, not all organizations adhere to a "golden rule" workplace philosophy as many frustrated employees and volunteers will tell you. People have different thresholds to tolerate such frustration, and some reach the point where passion for the mission and meaningful connection are no longer enough to convince them to stay. In other words, once engaged doesn't mean always engaged.

People don't stay committed to an organization when they:

- Feel overwhelmed with too many or conflicting management directives
- Don't understand what the organization is all about and what is expected of them
- Are afraid that their work isn't valued
- Don't see how the various parts of the organization connect in the "big picture"
- Don't share a sense of ownership in the organization, including being involved in solving problems and offering ideas.[7]

High turnover and low morale are signs of a disconnected, disengaged workplace run by clueless or complacent management. Managers who are disengaged themselves and show little concern for those they work with cannot expect their employees and volunteers to be enthusiastic and engaged. Staff and volunteers can tell whether management's concern for them is genuine or just lip service.

A few years ago I heard from a nonprofit professional who shared this negative experience. She and her colleagues were increasingly frustrated, discouraged, and disheartened about their work situation, which they described as "toxic." Managers issued multiple conflicting directives and set unrealistic expectations while providing little guidance or sufficient resources to enable staff to achieve their goals. They also paid little attention to staff concerns until a consultant was hired to address the issue of high turnover. In response to one of the consultant's recommendations, management set up a "suggestion box" system to solicit staff feedback and ideas. More than 135 suggestions were turned in the first week, and there were only 30 employees on staff!

Internal Marketing Tools of Engagement

Based on the 3 R's Foundation (Respect-Recognition-Reinforcement), each set of internal marketing tools will enable you to better engage your employees, volunteers, and (ultimately) your consumers by helping employees and volunteers clearly understand how their work impacts the organization's ability to move forward and fulfill its mission. These tool-sets work to connect your employees and volunteers on three fundamental levels by:

- **Connecting Staff/Volunteers to Your Organization** to ensure they know where they fit within the organization, what is expected of them, and how best to accomplish the mission and purpose
- **Connecting Staff/Volunteers to Your Consumers & Stakeholders** to ensure they understand who is important to your organization, what is important to them, and how best to serve them
- **Connecting Staff/Volunteers to Each Other** to ensure they understand their collective impact on the mission and how best to work together to achieve the organization's goals in pursuit of its mission.

The next three chapters provide ideas and examples of how you can apply each set of internal marketing tools to engage your employees, volunteers, and board members (as a special volunteer subset) by connecting them to your organization, to the people it serves, and to each other. Given the wide variation of nonprofit organizations and their operations, not all examples cited will be applicable in every instance. Where possible, I encourage you to be open to how you may be able to adapt some of the tools to your organization. You may also be familiar with some of the activities because you're already using them or have tried them in the past. In these cases, continue the activities that work for you and build on them where appropriate.

What if you're not in a position of authority to use these tools of engagement throughout your organization? What if you're unable to get management support? The good news is you can make an impact with internal marketing at a micro level – within a smaller department or division or sub-unit of your organization.

In situations where leadership is lacking and management is indifferent, you can still be proactive in engaging the staff and volunteers you work with by applying internal marketing. When you demonstrate respect for the people you work with and serve, when you positively recognize and reinforce their efforts in pursuit of the organization's mission, others in the organization will notice. They'll want to work with you and may even replicate your efforts to engage even more people, creating a halo effect. In other words, you can apply internal marketing despite management.

Endnotes

1. David Zinger, "Let's Co-Create an Employee Engagement Charter," The Employee Engagement Network, http://employeeengagement.ning.com/forum/topics/lets-cocreate-an-employee, accessed May 19, 2011.

2. Michael Lee Stallard: Insights on Leadership and Employee Engagement blog, "Rise of Lonely American Employees Undermines Productivity," June 13, 2011 http://www.michaelleestallard.com/rise-of-lonely-american-employees-undermines-productivity (accessed June 14, 2011).

3. Zinger, op. cit.

4. Jim Haudan, *The Art of Engagement*, McGraw-Hill, 2008, 17-25.

5. William Keenan, Jr., interview with Richard Axelrod, "The Art (and Science) of Engagement, " *Engagement Strategies Magazine*, Vol. 15, Issue 2, June/July 2011, 18.

6. Kristie Cattafi, "The NonProfit Times' 50 Best Nonprofits to Work for in 2011" (Medium Organizations), *The NonProfit Times*, April 2011, 19.

7. Jim Haudan, *The Art of Engagement*, McGraw-Hill, 2008, 31-70.

CHAPTER 5

Connecting to the Organization

"An aligned purpose and clear expectations are the foundation of an effective work environment. All good performance starts with clear goals. …Connect the dots between individual roles and the goals of the organization. When people see that connection, they get a lot of energy out of work. They feel the importance, dignity, and meaning in their job."

– Ken Blanchard and Scott Blanchard [1]

Take a moment to think back to when you were a new employee in a nonprofit. On your first day at work, how were you introduced to the organization? What was said about your role in it?

Perhaps you were given a job description, the mission statement, the annual work plan and the strategic plan. You were probably shown the location of your desk or office, the lunch room and where the restrooms were located. You were likely taken on a tour of your new workplace and introduced to senior staff and co-workers. You may have also been given an organizational chart.

Now reflect on your experience after you were no longer "new" to the organization. After being on the job for one or more years, how were you reminded of the organization's mission and goals? Were you regularly or periodically updated on where the organization was headed and what was expected of you? Or did you and your fellow employees have to figure it out for yourselves?

The sharing of basic information with employees and volunteers – mission, direction, strategy, and expectations of its people in pursuit of the organization's goals – doesn't always take place due to benign neglect or a lack of sufficient top-down communication. It may also result from nonprofits pursuing lofty missions with limited resources. Under constant pressure to do more with less, it's not unusual for staff and volunteers to be spread thin. Kathy Bremer, former board chair of the Georgia Center for Nonprofits describes the situation, "… because there is not a single 'bottom line' (e.g., profit), there can be multiple agendas operating at the same time."[2]

This may be standard operating procedure, but it can also lead to disaster when staff and volunteers become disconnected and then disengage from the organization. Think low morale, high turnover, and the investment in time and effort to constantly recruit new hires and volunteers. High turnover can also negatively impact your brand as supporters and donors wonder why you're unable to keep people.

The first set of internal marketing tools described in this book connects employees and volunteers to your nonprofit by creating and reinforcing a common understanding of the overall organization and highlighting their respective roles in it. These tools include sharing basic organizational information (i.e., framing the big picture), connecting new employees and volunteers with the organization, and keeping all staff and volunteers connected with your nonprofit on an ongoing basis.

Let's talk about what that means.

The Big Picture: What Staff and Volunteers Need to Know

To become engaged, people need to be shown a "line of sight" that enables them to better understand how their efforts and actions contribute to an organization's success. Here's a sample list of what your employees, volunteers, and board members need to know:

- Who your organization is and what it's all about – your mission, vision, and values
- How your organization came to be – your nonprofit's history, including when and why it was founded, its timeline, milestones, etc., as background and insight into your organization's culture and operations

- Where your organization is headed, how you intend to get there, and progress towards achieving your goals – your strategic and annual operating plans, available resources, and any plan modification or updates
- Where they fit within the organization's scope and what is expected of them – job or position descriptions, role clarification, and work guidelines that clarify how people can add value to the organization
- How effective they are in serving the organization and whether the organization values their individual and collective contributions – feedback mechanisms (formal and informal), performance evaluation criteria, acknowledgment, and recognition.

Sharing this "big picture" is an ongoing effort that does not start and end with new employee and volunteer orientation. New people brought in are typically introduced to the organization, whereas long term employees and volunteers may be overlooked because they already know about the organization. Yet these current staff and volunteers still need reminders of the mission, goals, and their respective roles since expectations of their work may become unclear over time; or their job responsibilities may have changed (but not their job descriptions); or they may have just "hunkered down" and lost sight of the big picture.

To keep everyone on the same page, the Northeast Regional Cancer Institute (NRCI) reinforces its mission to "ease the burden of cancer in Northeastern Pennsylvania" by reading it aloud at the start of all staff and Board/Executive Committee meetings. NRCI President Robert Durkin explained that reciting the mission was suggested by the organization's chair "as a means to remind participants that the discussions and actions that follow should all lead back to the mission."[3]

While an organization's mission may be steadfast, the world we operate in is not. Nonprofit goals and resources need to be adjusted in a fluid marketplace that brings changes in regulations, population (demographics and cultural shifts), the economy, and the environment. As the proverb says, "Man plans and God laughs." Nonprofits need to continually communicate with employees and volunteers to keep them informed about any changes in strategic direction or organizational capacity.

We'll explore how you can effectively connect and engage both your new and current staff/volunteers, including keeping everyone on the same page.

Making the Initial Connection

New employees and volunteers join a nonprofit with some prior knowledge and ready-made perceptions based on the interview or recruitment process, any previous experience with the organization, and word-of-mouth influence from other staff, volunteers, or consumers. They may also be anxious about how they'll fit in with the organization. Welcoming new staff and volunteers is a critical opportunity to make a good first impression in their first few days and weeks. This includes reinforcing their positive perceptions, correcting any misperceptions, and above all, validating their decision to join the organization.

To make a good first-impression experience, ensure the appropriate person or people are available to greet and warmly welcome new employees and volunteers on their first day. You don't want new arrivals left standing around the office waiting for someone to figure out what to do with them! Strategically determine who the new people should meet during their first week, such as supervisors, co-workers, and peer mentors or volunteers who are positive brand ambassadors. If possible, don't bring in a new staffer when his/her direct manager is out of town or unavailable as it may leave the new person feeling disconnected and without initial guidance.[4]

Here are my favorite conversation starters about organizational commitment you can use when pairing new staff and volunteers with internal brand ambassadors.

- Current staff/volunteers can ask the new people: *What is it about this organization that appealed to you and convinced you to work here* [as employees] *or get involved* [as volunteers]*?*
- New staff/volunteers can ask the current people: *What is it about this organization that keeps you here?*

In addition to a warm welcome, an effective orientation or on-boarding approach ensures new people are made to feel they are valued by your organization and prepared to help it move forward. While a nonprofit's size and available resources determine how expansive its orientation efforts are, the following information needs to be conveyed, at a minimum:

- The organization's mission, values, goals, who it serves, how it operates, where it's going, etc.
- The players involved, including senior management, support staff, Board of Directors, and volunteer committees
- Work flow and measurement such as organizational structure, who does what, how individual and collective efforts are evaluated, etc.
- The outlook for the organization – this is important for giving new employees and volunteers a broader perspective by addressing how the organization is positioned within its community or nonprofit sector; who its partners and competitors are; and any market or regulatory trends that may impact the organization and its resources.

You can share this critical information with new hires and volunteers with a combination of individual or group meetings (e.g., one-on-one meetings with key leaders/managers or structured orientation program) and an organizational handbook with operating policies and other pertinent information. For example, the Graduate Management Admissions Council displays photos with names, titles, email, and phone numbers in its organizational chart to make it easier for new staff members to get to know their co-workers and other key players inside the organization.[5]

A colleague who has worked for several nonprofits shared the best orientation experience she's had with her current organization. She was warmly welcomed her first day and given an information packet with an organizational chart. After touring the office building, most of the day was spent meeting with key department people. The "nitty gritty" details of getting her name badge, system log-in, and email set up had been taken care of ahead of time – allowing more time to get to know the people and organizational lay of the land. She was assigned a "buddy" in that first week as a "go to" person for any questions she had. Other staff members also stopped by her office to introduce themselves. This inclusiveness made a significant impact in making her feel welcome, connected, and part of the team.[6]

Whether your organization is starting a new orientation program or you want to improve your current one, one of the best places to start is by listening to the people who are already working with you. Talk with your employees and volunteers after they've been on the job for a period of time; e.g., six weeks, three months, or longer. You can learn from their experience and solicit their input by asking "What do you know now about our organization that you wish you had known when you started?" Their insight and ideas can help you create a more effective on-boarding experience to better connect new staff and volunteers with your nonprofit.

Corporate without class

The new guy
down the hall
needs to learn
how we do
things around here.
We'll train him
without a course
by rolling eyes,
banter at lunch, and
afternoon chocolate bribes.
He'll fit in,
won't make waves
and tread lightly
around cultural cubicles.

– David Zinger © 2011,
from *Assorted Zingers*,
used with permission[7]

Keeping *Everyone* Connected to the Organization

New employees receive a lot of attention when they join an organization. But even those who start off enthusiastic and excited about their work can become disillusioned over time. When do employees who have been around for a while get to be reminded of their fit in and contribution to the organization? Unfortunately, this may only occur once a year at performance review time … and we know how much people look forward to that process!

This is where ongoing internal communication plays a major role. Leaders and managers need to continually share progress updates on what is happening with the organization (based on external and internal factors) and what it means for the employees and volunteers. "Making progress in meaningful work" is a key indicator of engagement.[8]

Transparency is a critical component of internal communications. NRCI's Robert Durkin explains: "As a non-profit we should be open to sharing details about our workings – fiscal, operational, programming with all levels of Board, staff and volunteers. This may create some discomfort during challenging fiscal times (i.e., staff concerned about job security), but my view is that we are all in this together, and as such they should have access to germane information so as to allow for fair assessment of their professional standing/development/future."[9]

A sample of internal communications vehicles you can use to help keep everyone connected and "in the loop" includes:

- Staff meetings, volunteer meetings
- Internal memos and newsletters (print and/or electronic),
- All-employee forums, such as town-hall type meetings or videoconferences (depending on the size of the nonprofit)
- Special events such as an annual meeting, staff and/or volunteer retreat, appreciation program, etc.

The Jewish Family & Career Services of Atlanta (JF&CS) keeps employees connected by holding all-staff meetings following its monthly board of directors' meetings. These staff meetings are led by CEO Gary Miller in a "face-forward sharing of information" on board meeting results, updates on grants and upcoming events. He also welcomes new employees, acknowledges any who may be leaving, and takes the time to recognize staff members' personal milestones, such as weddings, births, graduations, special anniversaries, etc. Most of the more than 200 staff members attend these meetings; those unable to attend receive meeting minutes to keep them up to date.

In addition to these monthly all-staff meetings, JF&CS periodically hosts "Lunch & Learn" sessions to address employee topics of interest and major issues facing the organization. These sessions enable employees to understand the process, rationale and implications of major management decisions. Both the monthly all-staff meetings and Lunch & Learns reflect the JF&CS' commitment to keep its employees connected and engaged.[10]

Maintaining the employee-organization connection is also important during times of transition. Several years ago, Northampton Community College (NCC) was getting ready to experience a retirement wave and the institution was concerned about the impact of losing a number of its dedicated long-term staff. A group of Advancement & Marketing staff members took a proactive role as "Keepers of the NCC Culture" and set out to identify what was most distinctive and most valued about the institution's culture. They assembled and shared a list of value statements throughout the organization; e.g., "Helping students succeed is our #1 priority." And, "We prize tradition, but don't let it stand in the way of change."

This initiative to articulate and communicate NCC's cultural values was well received within the institution. "The Northampton Way" values statement was not only added to the school's orientation for new faculty and staff, it continues to be reinforced on an ongoing basis. This helps keep all employees focused and on the same page, regardless of whether they've been with the school for ten weeks, ten months, or ten years. According to Heidi Butler, NCC's Director of Public Information and Community Relations, "People sometimes chuckle about 'The Northampton Way,' but the values statement has deepened understanding of what makes the culture here distinctive and it has become a source of pride."[11]

Given the hectic pace of today's workplace, combined with resources stretched to the limit, it's easy to lose sight of the "big picture," especially when people are busy putting out the latest fires. That's why reinforcing the organizational connection is so critical – employees and volunteers are more easily engaged with an organization when they understand the mission and know what is expected of them, what they need to do, and how they are progressing.

It's at this point that I'm often asked, "How do you keep everyone informed and continually connected without contributing to information overload?" It is a challenge. If you want to know how your people feel about the volume and effectiveness of communication, ask them: Are you getting the information you need to know to do your work? ... What can our organization do to improve our internal communications?

Action Plan Starter Notes

Identify all activities and practices in response to the questions below, including any past practices that are still feasible. Ask staff and volunteers for their input as a springboard to discuss how to strengthen this connection.

Note: Depending on your situation, you may choose to address these questions separately for employees and volunteers.

1. In your experience, **what works to connect your new employees and volunteers to your organization?**

2. What works to keep current employees and volunteers connected to your organization?

3. What else might you do **to strengthen this connection?**

4. What doesn't work that you can **discontinue** doing?

Endnotes

1. Ken Blanchard and Scott Blanchard, "Do Your People Really Know What You Expect from Them?" *Fast Company* Expert Blog, July 18, 2011, http://www.fastcompany.com/1767714/do-your-people-really-know-what-you-expect-from-them (accessed July 20, 2011).

2. Kathy Bremer interview in "Marketing Research and Work in the Non-Profit World: Five Urban Myths," *The Marketing Dialog* blog, August 24, 2010, http://www.polarismr.com/TMD/bid/49797/Marketing-Research-and-Work-in-The-Non-Profit-World-Five-Urban-Myths (accessed August 26, 2010).

3. Robert Durkin, in an email to the author, July 27, 2011.

4. Alexandra Levit, "Make Sure Your New Person Doesn't Quit," *Alexandra Levit's Water Cooler Wisdom*, July 11, 2011, http://blog.alexandralevit.com/wcw/2011/07/make-sure-your-new-person-doesnt-quit.html (accessed July 18, 2011).

5. Pepe Carreras, Vice President, Marketing Operations, Graduate Management Admission Council, in an email to the author, February 21, 2012.

6. Author interview with Sarah Cooke, July 12, 2011.

7. David Zinger, *Assorted Zingers: Poems and cartoons to take a bite out of work*, Canada, 2011, 19.

8. Quoted in Derek Irvine, "Engage Employees by Helping Them See Meaning in Their Work," *Human Capital League* blog, August 5, 2011, http://humancapitalleague.com/Home/16923 (accessed August 5, 2011).

9. Robert Durkin, in an email to the author, July 27, 2011.

10. Author interview with Brenda Fiske, Chief Marketing Officer, Jewish Family & Career Services of Atlanta, Inc., January 11, 2012.

11. Heidi Butler, in an email to the author, December 5, 2011.

CHAPTER 6

Connecting to Customers

> Ensure all staff … as well as key volunteers have chances to deeply experience the programs and services of the organization and potentially even meet or observe beneficiaries. Only then will internal stakeholders really be able to articulate the magic of your organization's brand meaning.
>
> – Jocelyne S. Daw and Carol Cone [1]

The second set of internal marketing tools is used to establish customer understanding by your employees and volunteers. This understanding grows when you share customer information with staff and volunteers, find ways to connect them with your customers, and involve them in improving customer care. Connecting employees and volunteers with customers is critical because the more your employees and volunteers know about your customers, the better they can take care of them.

Share Customer Information

You can build this understanding among staff and volunteers by sharing basic, non-confidential information about your customers. The type and amount of detailed information will vary by employee and volunteer job level and responsibility; i.e., not all staff members and volunteers need to have equal access to such information. For example, a hospital volunteer will not have access to or need the same patient information as the medical practitioner treating the patient.

At a minimum, those who work in your organization need to know:

- Who your customers (and prospective customers) are – in terms of general demographic and/or behavioral characteristics.
- Why they are in need of your services/programs.
- How customers can get the most out of your programs/services, including what results they need to achieve to be successful in their interactions with you.

- How they chose or were referred to you.
- What they think about your organization.

Such customer information resides in various locations throughout a nonprofit. For example, general descriptions of customers and how they can benefit from an organization's programs may be found on your website ("who we serve"), in promotional literature (success stories and testimonials featured in the annual report), and in grant requests or fundraising campaign case statements. Information on referral sources and client service maximization are typically part of an organization's operations that may be found in staff/volunteer handbooks, with updates communicated via internal memos and/or at staff meetings. Customer feedback can be obtained formally in surveys or informally by observing and listening to customers.

Gathering and sharing this type of information – knowing the customers and stakeholders who are important to your organization and what is important to them – is part of communicating "the big picture" that helps connect employees and volunteers to your organization, as discussed in the last chapter. Sharing this customer information can be easily overlooked, especially with staff and volunteers who have minimal or indirect contact with your consumers. To gauge whether your people have sufficient customer knowledge, ask them what customer information they need to do their work and whether or not they have this information. Then follow up accordingly.

Creating customer understanding is more than a once-and-done effort. Environmental trends and changes may affect your customer base. For example, economic changes resulting in higher unemployment and more home foreclosures have increased the need for community and social service support for middle-class consumers.

This leads to the questions: *How often do your nonprofit customers change? How often do you convey this information to your employees and volunteers?*

Creatively Connect Staff and Volunteers to Your "Customers"

Provide opportunities, where appropriate, for your team to meet or visit the people served by your organization so they can better appreciate your mission-in-action.

Here is how several nonprofits make a face-to-face connection between customers and staff/volunteers, including those with limited or indirect customer contact.

- The Arthritis Foundation invites individuals living with arthritis to share their stories with employees at monthly all-staff meetings. This reminds Arthritis Foundation employees how important their work is to people with arthritis.[2] It also provides an opportunity for those consumers to connect with and publicly acknowledge staff efforts in the "prevention, control, and cure of arthritis and related diseases."[3]
- The Susquehanna River Valley Visitors Bureau is a small tourism promotional agency that relies on volunteers to work at its visitors centers. To help its volunteers become more knowledgeable about local events, the agency holds quarterly meetings for them and brings in guest speakers representing local tourist attractions to talk about their upcoming events or festivals. It also hosts several "fam" trips a year, taking its "volunteers to members throughout the tri-county region so they may have first-hand experience of members, events and tourism amenities in the area."[4]
- The Good Shepherd Rehabilitation Network, based in Allentown, PA, invites its hospital board members to help out at special events and outings with its wheelchair-bound residents, such as the Fish Fry (where residents fish in a stocked area of a local creek) and annual Christmas Brunch. Former Good Shepherd board member Cynthia Lambert

> shared her experience participating in these events. "As a board member, it exposed me to the most important element of our mission – the people we serve."[5]

Making a tangible connection between staff/volunteers and customers benefits all parties. Employees and volunteers get to see customers as real people, not just faceless names served by the mission. And customers get to associate a face or voice with the nonprofit and better understand the people behind the organization.

Involve Staff and Volunteers in Customer Care

Once your employees and volunteers have the information and connection they need to better understand customers, you can engage them in improving customer care. If you formally measure customer satisfaction, share the findings with employees (and volunteers when appropriate) so they know what your customers think about how you're doing. If you don't conduct such surveys, then periodically ask staff/volunteers to share what they observe and/or hear from their interactions with customers.

If survey results or anecdotal evidence suggests customer perceptions are positive, it's important to share this with staff and volunteers and recognize their efforts in taking care of customers. If the results point to the need for improvement, solicit employee input and ideas. It's important to talk with your own people – especially those on the frontline who are closest to your customers – before seeking outside help as "the insiders of an organization understand the stupidity of its traditions better than the outsiders."[6]

Don't wait until the situation deteriorates before seeking employee/volunteer input on improving customer care. In staff and volunteer meetings, you can ask: *"If you were head of this nonprofit (as CEO or board chair), what one or two things would you do to improve service or program delivery to our customers?"* Staff and volunteers feel valued and respected when managers proactively seek their input and sincerely listen to their ideas.

Customers and stakeholders feel the same when employees and volunteers listen to them, as I learned when I facilitated a customer roundtable discussion for a nonprofit client. The organization served developmentally disabled children and was trying to figure out how to get a better return on its annual gala as a major fundraising event. Rather than taking the conventional route of brainstorming with development staff and volunteers on how to get a better turnout, this nonprofit invited a group of local corporate-community relations professionals to a special roundtable to discuss their concerns. The group consisted of mid-to-senior level managers responsible for representing their companies in the community. They were also key in recruiting their company colleagues and executives to sponsor and attend a variety of fundraising events.

Client staff listened to the feedback from the roundtable session where participants shared their professional concerns and frustrations in working with the nonprofit community. The takeaway message was that these professionals were suffering from "black-tie burnout" given the amount of nonprofit dinner galas, silent auctions, charity tennis and golf tournaments held throughout the year – at least every weekend (or so it seemed). Participants asked for a calendar of events in advance out of respect for their time so they didn't have to scramble to recruit colleagues to fill banquet tables and participate in charity sports outings. They also requested nonprofits set and coordinate fundraising priorities to prevent multiple requests to sponsor events.

As a result of this feedback, the client decided to put its annual gala on hold for a few years while it determined other ways to raise funds and work with local companies. A most unanticipated and welcome result was the corporate-community professionals' positive response to the nonprofit who hosted the roundtable. They were most appreciative as it was the first time a nonprofit approached them as a collective group to ask about their professional concerns and frustrations, rather than just asking for more financial support.

By sharing relevant customer information with your employees/volunteers, creatively connecting them with customers, and engaging them in continually improving customer care, you effectively create a mindset where employees and volunteers can focus on *"How does what I do (in fulfilling/pursuing the mission) and how I do it impact our customers?"* Equally important, you reinforce the most meaningful connection with your nonprofit's mission and the people it serves.

Action Plan Starter Notes

Identify all activities and practices in response to the questions below, including any past practices that are still feasible. Ask staff and volunteers for their input as a springboard to discuss how to strengthen this connection.

Note: Depending on your situation, you may choose to address these questions separately for employees and volunteers.

1. In your experience, **what works to connect your employees and volunteers to your customers?**

2. What else might you do **to strengthen this connection?**

3. What doesn't work that you can **discontinue** doing?

Endnotes

1. Jocelyne S. Daw, Carol Cone, *Breakthrough Nonprofit Branding: Seven Principles to Power Extraordinary Results*, (Hoboken NJ: John Wiley & Sons, 2011), 114.

2. Author interview with Kimberly Beer, Associate Director, Advocacy, Arthritis Foundation, November 4, 2011.

3. Arthritis Foundation website: http://www.fightarthritispain.org/index.asp?L1=24 (accessed September 12, 2011).

4. Andrew Miller, Executive Director, Susquehanna River Valley Visitors Bureau, in an email to the author, June 24, 2009.

5. Author interview with Cynthia A. Lambert, August 26, 2011.

6. Andrew Filipowski quoted in *Pursuit of the Summit: Attracting and Retaining the Best Employees and Customers*, (Scottsdale, AZ: PowerNotes, 1999), 61.

CHAPTER 7

Connecting to Other Employees & Volunteers

> The [first] key … is having a highly skilled and credible staff who the volunteers respect. The second is to make sure the working relationships between the staff and volunteers are enjoyable.
>
> – John D. V. Hoyles [1]

This last set of internal marketing tools is the most overlooked. Employees and volunteers need to understand how, by working together and supporting each other's efforts, they can help an organization achieve its goals. When employees and volunteers understand how their work is interrelated, they have a greater appreciation for how their collective efforts contribute to the organization's success in advancing the mission.

Lucy Cabrera, president of the Food Bank of New York City, recognizes the importance of this connection. She explains: "There is a shared understanding that without everyone in the organization, we can't achieve our overarching goals. I've seen organizations where there is tremendous internal competition between areas because they don't have a common sense of direction. They fight over limited resources so they can advance a goal their area is working on. It is demoralizing and, in the end, minimizes outcomes."[2]

The need to connect employees and volunteers with each other applies to all nonprofits – regardless of how many employees and volunteers they have. Smaller nonprofits don't have as many organizational silos as their larger counterparts, but they can be just as insular. With fewer employees and volunteers, communications among and between them are taken for granted. The reality is these workers are expected to do a lot with few resources and are spread so thin that they don't always have the luxury of time or place to connect with each other.

This critical connection involves bridging internal divides to foster collaboration and support among and between your employees and volunteers. You can't fulfill the mission in a vacuum. It requires a strong sense of common purpose and teamwork – a "we're all in this together" mentality. Note: While forging this connection won't preclude internal squabbles, it can help minimize them and get everyone working together to move your organization forward.

In this chapter we'll look at some of the ways you can strengthen relationships and connect employees to employees, employees to volunteers, and volunteers to volunteers via:

- your mission
- links to the "bigger picture"
- intra- and interdepartmental information-sharing
- proactive internal communications.

This chapter also touches upon board members as a special group of volunteers and the "mirror" relationship between nonprofit employees and volunteers.

Highlight the Mission as Your Touchstone

At Volunteer Vancouver/Vantage Point, Executive Director Colleen Kelly reinforces the value of mission focus for employees and volunteers. She states, "[E]veryone understands they are in it for the same thing: to deliver the mission of the organization! Common purpose – one workforce."[3]

Here's an exercise you can use at your next staff and/or volunteer meeting or retreat that helps illustrate this common purpose. Distribute copies of your mission statement with yellow markers to everyone. Ask them to highlight what aspects of the mission their work impacts, and then have each person share the results. Discuss how their roles overlap and reinforce that despite having different jobs, everyone contributes to the mission.

Encourage Activities that Connect People to the Bigger Picture

- Nancy Lublin, CEO of DoSomething.org and founder of Dress for Success, wrote a book that shares what corporate America can learn from successful nonprofits. She describes the value of helping people get in touch with what their organizations are all about: "When your job description includes crunching numbers or pouring coffee, the larger purpose of your work isn't smack in front of your face. Lincoln Center gets those people out from behind their desks to witness a performance, providing them with tickets and event passes. … When an employee who works on the playbill, for example, can see the fruits of his labor in the hands of an actual audience member, his important role in the organization becomes real. That employee goes home feeling not only more cultured but also more empowered in his work. And he comes back to the office tomorrow, super motivated."[4]
- Recognizing that staff tended to silo themselves by the specific programs they were involved with, the leadership at ArtsMidwest set up an in-office day camp, complete with a campfire broadcast on TV and S'more snacks, where staff engaged in a program idea-exchange. "Camp Arts Midwest" was successful in pooling information from staff members and increased their social capital. David Fraher, Arts Midwest executive director, commented, "It was fascinating. People stopped

looking at each other as co-workers and saw each other as potential resources for new information."[5]

- Diane Pascal, Director of Development and External Relations, Inspiration Corporation, shares how her organization keeps staff members up to speed as it grows. According to Pascal, "We've developed a quarterly cross-volunteering program that requires staff to work in another program [other than the ones they work with daily]. We're very intentional and make sure everyone rotates. People volunteer to serve a meal, do mock interviews in our employment program, and then help organize a clothing closet. It builds understanding and respect for everyone's role. It keeps us feeling like a team."[6]

Encourage Departmental and Inter-Departmental Sharing at Staff Meetings

Regularly, or periodically as needed, invite employee representatives from different departments to attend each other's staff meetings so they know what's going on and can share what's happening in their respective areas. This is especially critical when one group's initiatives impact another group's work.

- At its weekly staff meetings, DoSomething.org asks each participant to share one accomplishment, one goal, and one request. Nancy Lublin explained: "The intention is for major departments and individuals to sync both priorities and pain-points [so] people have mutual awareness."[7]
- Volunteers across the organization also need opportunities to share their ideas and experiences with each other. A nonprofit colleague described how her organization encouraged volunteers

> "to know each other better, understand how the organization worked, and feel valued." She commented, "[We] would hold monthly meetings for volunteers, more as a reward than an operational requirement. Although we sometimes covered a few ops matters, they were primarily to bond and develop the volunteers. Each session included fun activities, good food and personal development – helping them in life and to do their volunteer work. [We] also included a small recognition for a specific volunteer or two who had done something extra or special. This gave them a chance to talk about their achievements, indirectly helping everyone understand what was going on in the group."[8]

In-person staff meetings are slowly disappearing as a primary medium for organizational communications due to electronic media's expedience. Yet such face-to-face gatherings – where people can hear, see, and provide instant feedback to the message as it is delivered – retain their value as a rich form of communication. Nonprofits need to manage communication effectiveness and efficiency. A guide to keep in mind is to match the message with the medium: the greater the message's importance and sensitivity, the greater the need for face-to-face communication.

Proactively Communicate within the Organization

Communication is the thread that connects everyone who works in and for your nonprofit. Its overall purpose is to enable and empower your employees and volunteers with the information they need to accomplish their work; effective internal communication also keeps them focused and engaged.

- Keep employees and volunteers informed of the organization's vision and direction. Nancy Lublin explains, "Nothing is more enervating, as an employee [or volunteer], than sensing you're not in the know, that you're purposely being excluded or even deceived by organizational leaders. It breeds disillusionment and distrust."[9] Another disturbing result is disengagement. Seriously, you can't expect employees and volunteers to carry out your mission and directives if you don't keep them in the communications loop!

- Share any operational/policy changes that impact employee and volunteer efforts. Communicate all changes in operations or policy openly, honestly, and in a timely manner. Include the rationale behind such changes so people better understand why a change has occurred and what is expected of them as a result of the change.
- Encourage and respond to feedback and ideas. Tap into employee and volunteer input on how to improve organizational efficiency and effectiveness. Asking for people's ideas shows you respect them. Regardless of how you seek their input – whether in regular or special staff meetings, town hall forums, annual retreats, surveys, a problem-solving project or idea-generating task force – it's critical that you respond. While it's unrealistic to be expected to implement every suggestion or recommendation that's offered, it is essential to acknowledge that input and explain why some ideas are practical and others are not. Employees and volunteers who feel their input goes into a communications black hole will stop speaking up and will disengage.

Despite senior management's best intentions to provide top-down communication (i.e., sharing strategy and plans, operational updates, policy changes, etc.), some managers and supervisors impede this flow of information by not passing it along to staff and volunteers in a timely manner or even at all. Perhaps these managers don't know what's expected of them in communicating to the people who report to them or they lack management communications training. There are also managers who tend to hoard information for power or control. Those unlucky enough to work for the latter type of manager will rely on the organizational grapevine for information. They'll do an end-run around their manager to get the scoop from colleagues whose managers do share information.

The danger of not communicating, regardless of the reason, is that employees and volunteers who feel they are kept in the dark will find a way to seek out the information they need. Whether the information they get is consistent with senior management's intended message is questionable. But that's the risk taken by organizations that don't invest in developing and reinforcing their managers' communications skills.

At the other end of the spectrum are managers unable to differentiate and prioritize "need to know" vs. "nice to know" information, so they overwhelm employees and volunteers by sharing it all. Nonprofits need to be sensitive to employee/volunteer workloads and time constraints in being able to absorb it all. How much is too much information? The best way to find out is to ask: What information is needed to carry out your work? How often? What's the best way to get this information? What feedback mechanisms do you need?

Nonprofits run solely by volunteers also face communication challenges. For example, TEAM Punta Gorda is an all-volunteer organization that works with "residents, business and property owners, and government officials to rebuild and revitalize the greater Punta Gorda" region in Florida.[10] It keeps its volunteers, partners, and the community-at-large connected through its master plan and annual plan; a variety of improvement projects and programs; improvement awards and volunteer recognition; fundraising events; and an annual meeting. The organization's website (www.teampuntagorda.org) is the primary communications vehicle that keeps volunteers, partners, and the public informed and engaged.

A Special Note about Board Members and Volunteers

Nonprofit board members are volunteers, yet they differ from most volunteers based on their scope of responsibility for the organization. The board's primary function may be strategic, advisory, operational, or some combination of all three, depending on the nonprofit. What most distinguishes board members from other volunteers is the board's responsibility for the organization – its members provide governance, fiduciary oversight, and strategic direction. In addition, they may be required to be donors and aid in fundraising. A board's executive committee – chairperson, vice-chair, secretary/treasurer, and past chair – are also responsible for hiring and evaluating the organization's executive director or chief executive officer.

Non-board volunteers typically serve in an operational and/or advisory capacity. They may also be recognized and developed for future board service (think volunteer farm team or talent pool), although some nonprofits select their boards from outside their volunteer corps. Regardless, since both groups share in their service to a nonprofit, their connection to each other should not be overlooked or taken for granted. To strengthen board-volunteer understanding, consultants Betty Stallings and Susan Ellis, co-authors of *Leading the Way to Successful Volunteer Involvement*, suggest board members:

- Spend time shadowing a direct service volunteer.
- Participate in volunteer recognition events where all volunteers are recognized as partners in the mission.
- Discuss the organization's approach to volunteer engagement in new board member orientation, including how the board supports volunteer involvement.
- Invite one or more volunteers to a board meeting to share their volunteer experience with the organization.

- Designate a board member position as liaison to volunteer engagement activities, such as serving on a volunteer management committee or as the key board contact with the staff member responsible for volunteers.[11]

A colleague of mine who has served on several nonprofit boards summed up his experience: "To me there is nothing like being around total strangers who share a common goal, join together on a board, and accomplish things – it's a wonderful feeling!"[12]

The Volunteer-Employee Relationship

How effectively your nonprofit forges and maintains these internal connections (employee-employee, employee-volunteer, and volunteer-volunteer) is a reflection of a workplace culture that influences people's perceptions of your nonprofit brand. There's a strong mirror-like link between employee and volunteer engagement: staff members who work closely with volunteers pay attention to how those volunteers are treated. Similarly, volunteers are sensitive to employee perceptions of the workplace. A once-loyal volunteer who became frustrated with the negative tension emanating from a nonprofit told me, "The organization seems to expect the volunteers to be a subset of their staff, and we know how poorly they treat their staff. So in retrospect, why do we expect them to treat us volunteers any differently?"

Keep in mind the way employees feel will impact how volunteers feel and vice-versa. If your employees and volunteers don't feel valued, neither will your customers, donors, and other key stakeholders!

Action Plan Starter Notes

This last connection involves creating and maintaining a collaborative culture among employees, volunteers, and board members. Identify all activities and practices in response to the questions below, including any past practices that are still feasible. Ask staff and volunteers for their input in discussing how to improve this connection.

1. In your experience, **what works to connect your employees, volunteers and board members to each other?**

2. What else might you do **to strengthen this connection?**

3. What doesn't work that you can **discontinue** doing?

Endnotes

1. John D. V. Hoyles, Canadian Bar Association, excerpt of his response to the question: "How does your association involve members in the work of your staff?" in the "CEO to CEO" column, *Associations Now*, March 2011, 53.

2. Joceylne S. Daw and Carol Cone, *Breakthrough Nonprofit Branding*, (Hoboken, NJ: John Wiley & Sons), 98.

3. Susan J. Ellis, *From the Top Down: The Executive Role in Successful Volunteer Involvement* (Philadelphia, PA: Energize, Inc., 2010), 111.

4. Nancy Lublin, *Zilch* (New York, NY: Portfolio, 2010), 15-16.

5. Samuel J. Fanburg, "Who Says Work Can't be Fun?" in *The NonProfit Times* "50 Best Nonprofits to Work for in 2011," April 1, 2011, 18.

6. Daw and Cone, op.cit., 120.

7. Nancy Lublin, op.cit., 152.

8. Erica Collins, in a LinkedIn discussion with the author (Consultants Network: HR & Change), July 25, 2011.

9. Nancy Lublin, op.cit., 15.

10. Author's interview with Bill Welsch, member of Team Punta Gorda's leadership team, September 30, 2011. http://www.teampuntagorda.org/index.html

11. Betty B. Stallings and Susan J. Ellis, *Leading the Way to Successful Volunteer Involvement*, (Philadelphia, PA: Energize, Inc., 2010), 174-175.

12. Merrill Dubrow, "Time to Find Out What Organizational Boards You Have Been On And How Was The Experience?", August 25, 2010, The Merrill Dubrow Blog, http://www.marcresearch.com/blogs/merrill/2010/08/25/time-to-find-out-what-organizational-boards-you-have-been-on-and-how-was-the-experience/ (accessed September 10, 2010).

PART 3

Facilitating Your Nonprofit Engagement

CHAPTER 8 - Keeping People Engaged

CHAPTER 9 - Making It Happen – Your Internal Marketing Plan

AFTERWORD

CHAPTER 8

Keeping People Engaged

> Successful brands are built by people … It starts with those closest to the organization – our employees, board, and volunteers. They are our ambassadors and reflect our brand in the workplace and community.
>
> – John Pfeiffer [1]

Effectively connecting your employees and volunteers to your organization, your consumers, and each other is critical to developing and maintaining an engaged workforce. This chapter explores several situations that can lead to disengagement and offers guidance on what you can do to help keep people engaged.

A Broad Mission and Increasing Workload Take a Toll

Meaningful work in support of a nonprofit's mission is essential to engaging employees and volunteers. It can also contribute to burnout. This may happen because many nonprofits have broad mission statements that let them justify responding to even remotely-related requests. The more diffuse the mission becomes – known as "mission drift" – the more difficult it is for a nonprofit to use its resources effectively for maximum impact.

Staff and volunteers who are truly passionate about the mission find it difficult to turn down any request or discontinue programs that are no longer cost-effective. For example, a young woman who worked for one of my nonprofit clients proudly reported during a staff meeting on a community support seminar she had organized and run the previous week. The seminar had sparse attendance. In discussing whether the event was worthwhile, she exclaimed, "But we helped the three people who came to this seminar!" Given the time and resources she invested in putting on this seminar, it was a noble effort but not a cost-effective one. To ensure continued viability, a nonprofit needs to consider the "return on investment" of its precious resources: manpower, time, and funds.

Another contributor to burnout happens when management keeps adding strategic directives without taking any away. Some nonprofit initiatives take on a life of their own, and management continues to automatically sink resources in these programs/

events/activities without stepping back to address "Why are we doing this? Is it still relevant to our mission and our market?" Jim Haudan, author of *The Art of Engagement*, says of this situation: "Leaders don't stop. Leaders don't remove. Leaders just add to the things they expect to be done, and then are surprised that people feel hopeless and disengaged."[2]

Adding projects and programs without taking any away leads to increased work pressure, information overload, and multi-tasking to keep up with it all. Overwhelming employees and volunteers in this way also negates the feeling of "making progress on meaningful work" – a key contributor to feeling motivated and engaged at work.[3] Is it any wonder that staff members and volunteers start to withdraw and disengage before they implode?

Consider these guidelines to maintain organizational focus and minimize escalating the volume of projects on an already stressed workforce:

- Before undertaking new initiatives, take the time to **STOP** and consider what you're asking of your employees and volunteers. For example: Are your new plans realistic, given your resources and capacity? Will your employees and volunteers be able to handle these new initiatives without undue burden?
- **FOCUS** your strategic intent by asking: What resources and/or trade-offs are necessary to undertake proposed initiatives? What, if any, current programs or activities can we give up? To help nonprofits prioritize their efforts, management consultant Peter Drucker recommended they assess existing program viability by asking:
  1. If we weren't already doing this [program, event, activity, etc.], if we weren't already committed, would we start doing this now?
  2. Is what we're doing still the right focus?[4]
- **LISTEN** and take into account employee ideas and concerns: Do employees and/or volunteers clearly understand your new direction and the rationale behind it? What ideas/suggestions do they have to effectively execute the new plan(s)?

Even in nonprofits with a clear purpose, disengagement is still possible due to external factors. Most nonprofit employees and volunteers are at risk during times of economic and political uncertainty as they struggle to meet growing mission-related needs with increasingly scarce resources. Continually being asked to "do more with less" and "work smarter, not harder" can lead to burnout.

Vera Walline, executive director of the Northeast PA Area Health Education Center, described her concern with the fiscal climate's impact on engagement: "When I get together with other nonprofit executive directors, we all look at a dismal funding future, and wonder how long we can hang on. Personally, I will continue to work to do the most with what we have, as long as we are funded, but I do sense exhaustion in my peers. While our board is wonderful about contacting legislators, I can't help but think that they would be more engaged if we weren't regularly threatened with a cut off of funds."[5]

How do you deal with this situation? While there's no one-size-fits-all solution for this (other than finding a magic lamp with a genie who can take care of your funding issues), it helps to engage your employees and volunteers in discussing coping strategies.

People Have to Matter as Much as the Mission

The difference in how volunteers and employees are treated on a daily basis depends on the management style of the person or people in charge. Are employees and volunteers recognized and respected for their roles in fulfilling the mission, or are they considered disposable commodities?

As mentioned at the end of the last chapter, your organizational culture influences public perceptions of your brand. It's difficult for nonprofits dealing with low morale and high turnover to maintain "share of heart." *How can an organization effectively engage consumers when it is unable to engage its own staff members and volunteers?*

Despite their well-intentioned commitment, employees and volunteers may become frustrated with a nonprofit organization and reach a point where passion for the mission and meaningful connection are no longer reason enough to stay. Remember, because people were once engaged doesn't guarantee they'll stay engaged.

Presuming a good hiring fit between employee (or volunteer) and the organization, most people start off excited about their work and eager to engage. But when they struggle to meet unclear or conflicting goals, or when they don't feel like they can make a difference, they begin to disengage. [Refer to Chapter 4 for a list of the reasons people disengage.] Dr. Judith M. Bardwick, who specializes in workplace psychology, explains: "When people are perceived as a cost and not a resource, when they are treated as a liability and not an asset, when no one seems to know or care that they are there, they don't work well, and they don't stay."[6]

What happens when employees don't feel valued? They disengage and leave the organization. Or worse, they disengage and stay. Neither scenario generates confidence in your internal (workplace) and external (public) brand. Disenchanted and/or disheartened employees do not make good brand ambassadors!

The same goes for volunteers who leave when they get frustrated and fed up. While it may seem easier for volunteers to exit since they're not held to an employment contract, that doesn't mean it's any less painful for them. According to author and leadership consultant Sally Helgesen, "Volunteers … work not for money but because they want to give back, make a difference, change the world. They work because they want to matter. Volunteers can, and will, quit the moment they feel undervalued."[7]

As the people behind the mission, your employees and volunteers are critical to your nonprofit's success. Yes, it takes continual effort to keep them connected and engaged with your organization, but the effort is well worth it. Sally Helgensen has found: "Eliciting superior performance from people requires making them feel as if they matter, as if they're contributing, as if they're making a difference. … Only an inspiring, trustworthy, respectful, and inclusive leader can attract and retain volunteers over the long run."[8] The same can be said of employees.

Successful nonprofit leaders take a proactive approach to managing their employees and volunteers. Both groups require:

- **an investment of time** for training and ongoing communication
- **attention** in terms of feedback and recognition
- **and the tools** (applicable resources) needed to accomplish the organization's goals and advance its mission.

These efforts form the foundation of internal marketing: Respect, Recognition, and Reinforcement. Applying these 3 Rs enables you to build and maintain an engaged workforce of employees and volunteers who are connected to your organization, your consumers, and each other. A strong "connection culture" reinforces a sense of common purpose, a sense of belonging, and a sense of being part of something special – these are the roots of employee and volunteer engagement that foster consumer engagement with a nonprofit brand.

There's nothing particularly difficult about strengthening these connections. Unfortunately, while internal marketing's premise is easy to grasp, its practice is easy to overlook. So take care of your employees and volunteers and they'll take care of your consumers and your brand.

Special Note on Managing Your Own Engagement

While management is responsible for a workplace culture that fosters employee and volunteer engagement, everyone in the organization is responsible for his or her own engagement. Following an organizational change in direction or leadership, if you find yourself becoming disenchanted and starting to disengage, it's time to perform a reality check. Talk discreetly with colleagues you respect for ideas on how best to address the situation. You may find that others have found themselves in a similar experience and may have advice to share.

Ultimately you need to ask yourself whether or not it makes sense to continue your service to a nonprofit – whether as employee, volunteer, or leader. Do you feel strongly enough about the mission that you're willing to adjust your expectations to continue to serve? Or is there another way you can support the mission in a different capacity?

If you're discouraged to the point that you can no longer tolerate the situation, then gracefully resign and regroup. Give yourself a breather … then find another worthwhile organization that's a better fit with your talent and passion.

Endnotes

1. Jocelyne S. Daw and Carol Cone, *Breakthrough Nonprofit Branding,* (Hoboken, NJ: John Wiley & Sons, 2011), 120.

2. Jim Haudan, *The Art of Engagement*, (New York, NY: McGraw-Hill), 32.

3. Daniel H. Pink, "Why progress matters: 6 questions for Harvard's Teresa Amabile," August 9, 2011, http://www.danpink.com/archives/2011/08/why-progress-matters-6-questions-for-harvards-teresa-amabile (accessed November 14, 2011).

4. Constance Rossum, *How to Assess Your Nonprofit Organization with Peter Drucker's Five Most Important Questions – User Guide,* The Drucker Foundation Self-Assessment Tool for Nonprofit Organizations (San Francisco, CA: Jossey-Bass, 1993), 33.

5. Vera Walline, in an email to the author, October 28, 2011.

6. Dr. Judith M. Bardwick, cited in "Addressing Today's Psychological Recession" in *Executive Matters*, The Member Newsletter of the American Management Association, January 2008, http://www.leadernetworks.com/downloads/exec-matters-jan08.pdf.

7. Sally Helgesen, "Why Mattering Matters," *Shine a Light*, Leader to Leader Institute, 2005, 56.

8. Ibid., 2005, 57.

CHAPTER 9

Making It Happen

> When you get right down to the meaning of the word 'succeed,' you find that it simply means to follow through.
>
> – F. W. Nichol [1]

At this point, you have an idea of what internal marketing tools you need to better engage your employees and volunteers. Now what? How do you apply this information to your organization?

This chapter is designed to help you put your ideas into a manageable internal marketing plan for engagement that fits your nonprofit. "Manageable" is the operative word here, as it is easy to feel overwhelmed given most nonprofit employee workloads. (*"Oh no, not another unrealistic plan that's a waste of time!"*) If you completed any of the Action Plan Starter Notes in this book, you've jump-started your internal marketing planning. If you haven't worked on them yet, set aside the time to do it. You can build on these notes to focus and prioritize your efforts using the special summary worksheets at the end of this chapter. These worksheets will help you develop a small number of attainable activities and initiatives, rather than a long list of "to do" items.

A Special Note About Research

You're encouraged to identify what internal information is available or might be needed to guide your internal marketing. For example, does your nonprofit survey employees and volunteers to assess their perceptions of the workplace, including what organizational practices support or impede their engagement? These research results (via surveys or focus groups) will also help you identify which, if any, segments of employees and volunteers need the most attention.

In addition to employee research, do you survey your customers or key stakeholders to understand their satisfaction or frustration with your nonprofit? This gives you "voice of the customer" insight that validates which aspects of the customer experience need to be addressed.

It's helpful to have both internal (employee-volunteer) and external (customer) research to support your efforts. However, don't let the absence of this research or lack of a research budget keep you from moving ahead with internal marketing. You may be able to find a research firm willing to help you on a pro-bono basis.

Tips for Successful Planning & Implementation

The following guidelines for successful planning and implementation will help you maximize your internal marketing.

1. Get others involved. Try to enlist the support of other people within your organization in internal marketing. The goal is to get buy-in from key staff members in administration, operations, client or member services, programming, development, human resources, marketing, etc. – whatever functional areas you think need to be involved. The more internal allies, the better.

Given the reality of internal politics, however, don't despair if you're unable to build broader involvement. Equally important, don't let others' unwillingness to participate prevent you from moving forward with internal marketing. If you're unable to initiate it on a "macro" level, throughout the organization, you can still have impact on a "micro" level by applying internal marketing tools of engagement within your own department or operational unit. When people begin to notice that your employees/volunteers are more engaged, more managers will be interested in how you're making that happen.

2. Keep the planning process simple. Yogi Berra once said, "You've got to be very careful if you don't know where you're going, because you might not get there."[2] His comment underscores the importance of creating a plan as a practical roadmap to guide your efforts. When developing your internal marketing plan, however, it's not necessary to engage in an extensive planning effort that produces nothing more than a three-inch binder that sits on a bookshelf and collects dust. The purpose of planning is to provide direction and stimulate action, not just to create a planning document. It doesn't matter if you draft your plan on a napkin at lunch – as long as it's something you'll use!

Consider a special staff meeting or mini-retreat to develop an internal marketing plan – ranging from several hourly sessions to a half-day or full day or whatever time you think is needed. Seclude yourself in a conference or meeting room. Better yet go off-site for this planning, if you can afford it, to allow for maximum participation without workplace interruptions. If budget is an issue, consider finding low-cost or free meeting space such as a conference room at a public library or community center.

Try to build some fun into your planning with creative ice-breakers or low-cost theme-related items. Here are several examples:

- At the outset of your planning session, ask participants what celebrity they would most like to have volunteer in your organization and how that person could best be engaged; then relate the discussion back to current engagement efforts.
- Distribute fortune cookies and ask participants how the fortune relates to engagement within your nonprofit. Or you can ask them to write a one-line fortune-saying that reflects the results of a successful internal marketing initiative.
- Give each participant a small pocket mirror (from a dollar-store or retail party outlet) as a symbol that what they see in the mirror reflects what your customers and community see; i.e., it's how people picture your organization.

Note: any creative exercise, theme, or token items you include in a planning session must relate to what you're trying to accomplish. You don't want to waste the group's time or energy with gratuitous activities! In addition, don't forget to bring in refreshments to help fuel the planning process.

3. Introduce internal marketing carefully. Because engagement is not a once-and-done effort, internal marketing is best implemented gradually or in small doses. Introducing it as a separate initiative or campaign may result in people giving it cursory acceptance as a "program-of-the-month." Internal marketing tools of engagement are most effective when integrated into an organization's operations on an ongoing basis. This doesn't mean, however, that you can't brand special elements of internal marketing. As mentioned in previous chapters, the Jewish Family & Career Services of Atlanta (JF&CS) hosts periodic "Lunch & Learn" sessions in which employees and managers discuss topics and issues that affect the organization. JF&CS also recognizes volunteers in a "Volunteer Spotlight" column featured in its monthly e-newsletter.[3]

Action Plan Summary Worksheets

To create your customized internal marketing plan, complete the following worksheets using the results of your Action Plan Starter Notes. Where applicable, identify any action-oriented items from your notes that can be implemented immediately.

Worksheet 1: Nonprofit Marketing and Engagement

Review your Action Plan Starter Notes in chapters 1-3 and respond to the following questions:

1. Considering **what's realistically do-able** given your organization's resources, **in what ways can your marketing efforts be improved?**

2. What can be done to **improve your customers' service experience**, including **ensuring consistency** among all brand touch points?

3. How will your organization **facilitate employee and volunteer engagement** via:

- **Respect?**
- **Recognition?**
- **Reinforcement?**

Consider what efforts in these areas currently work and what else needs to be done.

Based on your responses to the previous three questions, prioritize your efforts and be as specific as possible:

4. **Which three actions will you focus on** within the next several weeks/months?

5. When/how do you plan to **address the remaining actions?**

Worksheet 2:
Marketing Tools of Engagement

Review your Action Plan Starter Notes in chapters 5-7. List up to three action steps that your nonprofit needs to take to strengthen each of the following connections:

1. Your employees and volunteers → **your organization**

2. Your employees and volunteers → **your customers**

3. Your employees and volunteers → **each other**

Based on your responses to the previous three questions, prioritize your efforts and be as specific as possible:

4. **Which three actions** – within or among the connections – **will you focus on** within the next several weeks/months?

5. When/how will you **address the remaining actions?**

Worksheet Addendum: Internal Marketing Plan Implementation

You're almost done with your planning!

This worksheet covers several critical, yet often overlooked keys to effective implementation. Now that you have identified and prioritized your actions in (one or both of) the previous worksheets, it's important to consider the following:

1. How will you manage this plan? Specify when/how often you will monitor your progress.

2. How will you communicate the plan? Identify:

- Who needs to know about this plan?
- How you will introduce it?
- When/how often you'll share interim results?
- What communications vehicles you'll use?

3. How will you celebrate your plan? Specify when and how you'll recognize and celebrate people's individual and/or collective success in implementing the plan.

Napkin futures

Tabling strategy.
Gel pens drawn
during fast food lunch
sparking napkin artistry.
Ink bleeds
arrows, word, and stick figures
into thin paper.
Absorbing both
strategic thinking
and mustard drips
oozing from the overflowing cheeseburger.
It is going to be a good year.

– David Zinger © 2011,
from *Assorted Zingers*,
used with permission[4]

Endnotes

1. F. W. Nichol (n.d.). FinestQuotes.com. Retrieved December 23, 2011, from FinestQuotes.com Web site: http://www.finestquotes.com/author_quotes-author-F. W. Nichol-page-0.htm

2. Things People Said, "Yogi Berra Quotes," http://www.rinkworks.com/said/yogiberra.shtml (accessed December 23, 2011).

3. Author interview with Brenda Fiske, Chief Marketing Officer, Jewish Family & Career Services of Atlanta, Inc., January 12, 2012.

4. David Zinger, *Assorted Zingers: Poems and cartoons to take a bite out of work*, Canada, 2011, 19.

AFTERWORD

Can you think of anything more permanently elating than to know that you are on the right road at last?

– Vernon Howard [1]

Creating positive share of mind and heart for your nonprofit brand starts within your organization. People's perceptions of your nonprofit and the degree to which they'll engage with it (if at all) are greatly influenced by the individual and collective actions of everyone who works in your organization. To customers, donors, and other stakeholders, your employees and volunteers are the very embodiment of your brand.

The concept of internal marketing isn't difficult to comprehend in theory. However, what seems to be logic and common sense – take care of your employees and volunteers, and they'll take care of your customers – doesn't necessarily translate into common practice. This is why I encourage you to be intentional and proactive with internal marketing. By engaging your employees and volunteers as brand champions, you can build your organizational strengths and market advantage.

Special Note

The tools of engagement described in this book are important components of internal marketing, but they are not exhaustive. The tools include any and all programs, events, activities, and internal communications that reinforce the importance of your customers, donors, stakeholders, etc., and the employees and volunteers who serve them.

You can find more internal marketing ideas and inspiration in the resources list provided at the end of this book. I invite you to periodically visit my internal marketing & communications blog,

www.QualityServiceMarketing.blogs.com,

to learn what other organizations are doing, share your nonprofit's experiences, and stay in touch with me.

I wish you all the best in building your organization's share of mind and heart with internal marketing tools of engagement!

Endnotes

1. Vernon Howard, http://www.brainyquote.com/quotes/authors/v/vernon_howard.html (accessed January 24, 2012).

RESOURCES

Following are recommended books and websites for more information on nonprofit marketing, employee engagement, and volunteer engagement.

Books

Breakthrough Nonprofit Branding: Seven Principles to Power Extraordinary Results, by Jocelyne S. Daw, Carol Cone, Kristian Darigan Merenda, and Anne Erhard, John Wiley & Sons, 2011. Features great examples of nonprofit branding and re-branding.

Zilch: The Power of Zero in Business, by Nancy Lublin, Portfolio, 2011. Describes what for-profit companies can learn more nonprofits – also helpful for nonprofits.

From the Top Down: The Executive Role in Successful Volunteer Involvement (3rd edition), by Susan J. Ellis, Energize, Inc., 2010. Comprehensive guide on developing and implementing volunteer engagement strategy.

Leading the Way to Successful Volunteer Involvement, by Betty B. Stallings with Susan J. Ellis, Energize, Inc., 2010. Companion toolkit to *From the Top Down* with helpful worksheets and checklists.

Re-Engage: How America's Best Places to Work Inspire Extra Effort in Extraordinary Times, by Leigh Branham and Mark Hirschfeld, McGraw-Hill, 2010. Draws on extensive data from the "Best Places to Work" research to identify and apply the drivers of employee engagement in today's challenging times.

The Art of Engagement: Bridging the Gap Between People and Possibilities, by Jim Haudan, McGraw-Hill, 2008. Provides a framework for connecting organizational strategy and execution based on the root causes of engagement and disengagement.

Robin Hood Marketing: Stealing Corporate Savvy to Sell Just Causes by Katya Andresen, Jossey-Bass, 2006. Great book about nonprofit marketing.

Websites

http://employeeengagement.ning.com – The Employee Engagement Network hosted by David Zinger.

http://www.energizeinc.com/ener/ener.html – Susan Ellis's Energize website for leaders of volunteers.

www.nonprofitmarketingblog.com – Katya Andresen, *Robin Hood Marketing* author's blog.

www.qualityservicemarketing.blogs.com – Quality Service Marketing's blog on internal marketing & communications and nonprofit marketing. *Volunteer Engagement* e-book by Sybil F. Stershic (2010) also available for free download.

INDEX

A

Action Plan Starter Notes ix, 11–14, 25–29, 44–45, 67–69, 78–79, 92–93
  introduction 11–14

Action Plan Summary Worksheets 111–117

Arthritis Foundation 75

ArtsMidwest 85

Axelrod, Richard 52

B

Bardwick, Dr. Judith M. 102

Berra, Yogi 108

Blanchard, Ken 57

Blanchard, Scott 57

BlessingWhite, Inc., research 34

Board of Directors
  as volunteers 90–91
  functions and responsibilities 90–91
  initial connection and orientation 63
  relationships with employees 90–91

Brand
  awareness and meaning 22–23
  contacts and touch points 23–24, 33
  power 8–9
  responsibility for 9–11
  service equates with 17

Bremer, Kathy 59

Burnout 99–100

Butler, Heidi 67

C

Cabrera, Lucy 83

Callahan, Emily 31

Carlzon, Jan 39

Communication
  big picture 37, 53, 60–62, 67, 74
  encouraging departmental and inter-departmental sharing 86
  internal 65–67, 84, 86–89
  interpersonal skills training 40
  part of Respect (3 Rs) 37–39
  proactively 87–89

Cone, Carol 71

Connections
connection culture 51–52
encouraging departmental and inter-departmental sharing 86–87
keeping everyone connected 65–67
making the initial connection 62–64
sharing non-confidential information 73–74
tools of engagement 54
to customers 71–80
to other employees and volunteers 81–92
most overlooked of the tool-sets 83
to the organization 57–70

Customers
involving staff and volunteers with 76–78
perspective, what's important to 19–22
semantics 7–8
service experience 19–21
sharing non-confidential information with employees 73–74

D

Daw, Jocelyne S. 71
Disengagement 53
DoSomething.org 85, 86
Dress for Success 85
Drucker, Peter 6, 100
Durkin, Robert 61, 65

E

Ellis, Susan 90, 124
Employee-Customer Link 51

Employees
customer care 76–78
disengagement 53
employee-customer link 51
engaging, using the 3 Rs strategy 37–44
sharing non-confidential customer information with 73–74

Empowerment, part of Respect (3 Rs) 40–41

Engagement
connections 52–54
description 34
disengagement 53
includes employees and volunteers 34
managing your own 103–104
plan for making it happen 107–110
responsibility for 52
tips for planning and implementation 108–109

Enlisting support within your organization 108

F

Fiske, Brenda 42
Focus 100
Fogel, Elaine 11
Food Bank of New York City 83
Fraher, David 85

G

Georgia Center for Nonprofits 59
Good Shepherd Rehabilitation Network 75

Goodwill Industries 5–7, 43
Graduate Management Admissions Council 64

H

Haudan, Jim 100
Helgesen, Sally 102
Howard, Vernon 119
Hoyles, John D. V. 81

I

Inspiration Corporation 86

Internal Marketing
- cross-functional responsibility for 36
- definition 35–36
- inside-out marketing 35
- intentional 121
- internal marketing plan ix, 107-111
- introduce internal marketing carefully 110
- levels of understanding 35–36
- the Three Rs Formula 37–44
- tips for planning and implementation 108–109
- tools of engagement 54

Internal service culture 51

J

Jewish Family & Career Services of Atlanta 41–42, 66, 110

K

Keeping the planning process simple 108–109
Kelly, Colleen 84
Kotler, Philip 3, 6

L

Lambert, Cynthia 75–76
Lessons from work with nonprofits viii
Lincoln Center 85
Lublin, Nancy 85, 86-87

M

McEwen, Bill 34
Miller, Gary 66

Mission
- communicating 37–38, 59–61, 78
- highlighting 84-85
- maintaining organizational focus 100
- over-broad, contributing to burnout 99–100
- passion for viii
- people have to matter as much as 101–103
- pursuit via marketing 6–7
- unique role in nonprofits 33

N

Nardizzi, Steven 52
National Crime Prevention Council 9
Nichol, F. W. 105

Nonprofit Marketing
- differentiation 6–7
- how different from product marketing 17–18
- how the same as product marketing 22–24
- purpose 6
- responsibility for 9–11
- scope 9

Northampton Community College 66–67
the Northampton Way 67
Northeast PA Area Health Education Center 101
Northeast Regional Cancer Institute 61

O

Organizational culture 51, 91, 101, 103
Orientation *39, 63*

P

Pascal, Diane 86
People
have to matter as much as the mission 101–103
who are served by nonprofits (consumers and customers) 8
who work in nonprofits (employees and volunteers) 7–8
Pfeiffer, John 97
Product knowledge. *See* Training

Q

Quirk, Bill 38

R

Recognition (3 Rs) 37, 41–42, 43–45, 51, 54–55, 103, 112
Reinforcement (3 Rs) 37, 42, 45, 51, 54, 103, 112
credibility and consistency 43
Research 107–108
Resources
books 123–124
websites 124
Respect (3 Rs) 37–41, 44–45, 51, 54, 103, 112
elements of: explaining, training, and refraining 41

S

Schultz, Don E. 15
Schultz, Heidi F. 15
Services marketing 17–18
Service quality evaluation 19–22
Share of heart, meaning 6
Share of mind, meaning 6
Stallings, Betty 90
Susquehanna River Valley Visitors Bureau 75

T

TEAM Punta Gorda 89
Tools of Engagement 54–55
Training
interpersonal skills 40
part of Respect (3 Rs) 39–40
product knowledge 39
training checklist 39–40

V

Volunteer Vancouver/Vantage Point 84

Volunteers
- board members as 90–91
- customer care 76–78
- engaging, with the 3 Rs 37–44
- volunteer-employee relationship 91

W

Walline, Vera 101

Worksheets
See Action Plan Starter Notes
- Action Plan Summary Worksheets 111–117

Wounded Warrior Project 52

Y

YOUTH ARC – Youth Organized & United To Help the Association for Retarded Children vii

Z

Zinger, David 49, 118, 124

ABOUT THE AUTHOR

A respected thought leader on engaging employees through internal marketing, Sybil Stershic is the author of *Taking Care of the People Who Matter Most: A Guide to Employee-Customer Care.* She shares her expertise in her Quality Service Marketing blog where she also interviews experts and provides insight into the best ways to gain share of mind, share of heart.

Sybil is an accomplished speaker and business professional who helps service providers strengthen employee-customer relationships. She founded Quality Service Marketing in 1988, specializing in internal marketing and mission-focused/customer-focused staff development. She also teaches marketing fundamentals and conducts workshops nationwide for nonprofit and corporate managers.

In addition to her professional work, Sybil has been active as a volunteer leader in local and national nonprofit organizations, including serving as Chair of the American Marketing Association.

For more information, please visit:

www.QualityServiceMarketing.com.